SOMMER 14: A DANCE OF DEATH

Rolf Hochhuth

SOMMER 14: A DANCE OF DEATH

Translated by Gwynne Edwards

OBERON BOOKS
LONDON

WWW.OBERONBOOKS.COM

This edition first published in 2014 by Oberon Books Ltd
521 Caledonian Road, London N7 9RH
Tel: +44 (0) 20 7607 3637 / Fax: +44 (0) 20 7607 3629
e-mail: info@oberonbooks.com
www.oberonbooks.com

A catalogue record for this book is available from the British
Library.

PB ISBN: 978-1-78319-183-3
E ISBN: 978-1-78319-682-1

Cover design by

'The dead are among us, they are inside us. They ask us questions and demand of us that we answer for our crimes. What do we say to the little Jewish boy with the serious face who is on his way to the gas chamber, when we look to our current circumstances?'

Otto Schily, *Thoughts on Germany*, 1988

Characters

A WAR WIDOW

MAJOR DRAGUTIN DIMITRIJEVIĆ
leader of the Black Hand

TRIFKO GRABEŽ
member of the Black Hand

A GIRL

KAISER WILHELM II

GRAND ADMIRAL ALFRED VON TIRPITZ
Secretary of State of the Imperial Naval Office

GENERAL HELMUTH VON MOLTKE
Chief of General Staff

PROFESSOR WILLY STÖWER
artist

LIEUTENANT ERNST VON WEIZSÄCKER
an Officer

BARON WLADIMIR GIESL VON GIESLINGEN
Austro-Hungarian Minister to Serbia

BARON NICHOLAS GENRIKHOVICH HARTWIG
Russian Ambassador to Serbia

DIRECTOR OF THE WASHINGTON NATIONAL
GALLERY OF ART

HENRY STIMSON, *a politician and industrialist*

MISS MARGOT STIMSON, *his daughter*

A LUSITANIA VICTIM

CLARA IMMERWAHR HABER, *a scientist*

FRITZ HABER, *also a scientist*

*Servants, guests and bystanders
played by members of the company.*

The action takes place on the Isle of the Dead, a barren strip of land also known as 'no-mans-land' and in flashback to events in various palaces and diplomatic offices around Europe.

Prologue
The Isle of the Dead
Death

Scene 1:
The Madness of Murder
Paris, office of the Editor-in-Chief
of Le Figaro
16 March 1914
Clerk
Monsieur Gaston Calmette
Madame Henriette Caillaux
Secretary
Editor 2
Editor 3
Monsieur Joseph Caillaux

Song of the Scythes

Scene 2: King Edward Fails
The Imperial Burgtheater, Vienna
March 1909
Emperor Franz Joseph
King Edward VII of England
Mrs Alice Keppel
Princess Stéphanie

The Lemming Song

Scene 3:
His Majesty's Master Spy
The Reich Chancellery, Berlin
May 1914
Theobald von Bethmann-
Hollweg
Gottlieb von Jagow
Dr Theodor Wolff

The Espionage Song

Scene 4: Churchill's Bait
The Deck of the RMS Lusitania
March 1914
Lord Admiral Winston
Churchill
Lord Alfred Booth
Lady Jennifer Randolph-
Churchill

The Blood Pump

Scene 5: Shots in Sarajevo
A Viennese Cafe
28 June 1914
Major Dragutin Dimitrijevi
Trifko Grabež
A Girl

Death as a Teacher

Scene 6: Kaiserweather
Deck of the Imperial SMY
Hohenzollern
28 June 1914
Kaiser Wilhelm II
Grand Admiral Alfred von
Tirpitz
General Helmuth von Moltke
Professor Willy Stöwer
Lieutenant Ernst von
Weizsäcker

Intermission

INTERVAL

A Chorale of Balances

Scene 7: The Ultimatum
Austrian Embassy in Belgrade
10 July 1914
Baron Vladimir Giesl von
Gieslingen
Baron Nicholas Genrikhovich
Hartwig

Monologue of a Sophisticated
Munitions Manufacturer

**Scene 8: American
Dollars for Blood**
*The new wing of the Washington
National Gallery*
4 May 1915
Director of the Washington
National Gallery
Henry Stimson
Miss Margot Stimson

*One Gone Down with the
Lusitania*

Death in an Airship

Scene 9: A Scientist Fails
Faradeyweg 8. Dahlem, Berlin
Clara Immerwahr Haber
Fritz Haber

Do Not Obey

**Scene 10: Now Thank We
All Our God**
Ministry of War, Berlin
4 August 1914
General Helmuth von Moltke
Theobald von Bethmann-
Hollweg
Gottlieb von Jagow
Kaiser Wilhelm II
Grand Admiral Alfred von
Tirpitz
Dr Theodor Wolff
Professor Willy Stöwer

The Unknown Soldier

Nekrologue
The Isle of the Dead

This text went to press before the end of rehearsals and so may differ slightly from the play as performed.

PROLOGUE
ISLE OF THE DEAD

The music swells, organ-like, screaming, terrifyingly loud, even before the curtain rises.

A space, no-man's-land, a skull-grey strip, wide enough for the performance of the scenes of human interaction from the pre-war era, and for the appearances of DEATH in which he comments on these scenes. DEATH's presence remains in the background. Just as a worldly prince would observe the performance of a touring theatrical company before his castle, so here this gentleman, or lady – for DEATH is androgynous – watches the shadows of those fools, the arrogant and the abused, who in the Europe of 1914 backed themselves into the First World War with political games.

This war proved too much for DEATH. We will hear him explain.

The sounds of war mix with the unearthly music. From the smoke and bloody mud of the field rises a young German soldier, recently dead. He approaches the audience, taking each and every one of them in. DEATH inhabits his body. He takes a moment to acknowledge his new form and his surroundings before returning to the audience...

DEATH: Can you hear it?
    Humanity calls me
    I'm preparing for war
    Nine million people on the fields of the dead
    Nine million slaughtered,
    Few will survive.
    Some born in palaces, some born in slums
    Only the sons of kings will be spared.
    Victor and vanquished all equal as corpses.

    Nine million bodies paving the roads!
    A hundred thousand ninety times falling.
    And all those who warn against starting this slaughter
    Will be murdered or silenced, defeated.

    God ignores
    My reluctance!
    Makes me kill them by numbers,
    They shall die, yes. But I must escape,

This killing in thousands –
Does he think I'm machine?
I must flee or be snuffed out
Let someone else do the work!
I am Death, not Overkill!
If God wants them dead, he can do it without me!
I'm no mass murderer.
I take one by one.
But this is extinction by heavy industry!

Nine million, nine million then their sons
Like their fathers,
Will wage war again twenty years later!
Bloody revenge.
And this Second World War
Will kill six times the number.
Sixty million. Who would want
Nations to be so insane?
But the record-breaker?
World War Three.
What they burn the world with
Will consume the whole planet.
Apocalypse
Like it began, from a fireball,
The earth born in flames.
In death it will be so again.

And here's the inception that leads to the end
The hellish machine kicks into life
Humans themselves are making this happen
Men enact many good things.
Yet the evil they do leads to hellish destruction.

Where does it come from?
When the crowd crows, men go to war.
But those who are the cause of the carnage
Will always die peacefully in their beds.
A man's child perishes
His wife, starves to death,
And people say it's God's will?
Man thinks he's made in God's image,

But this self-slaughter
Must be man's true nature
Surely God is not thus afflicted
Surely this bloodlust is straight from the beast.

I must go and see
I must understand it
God has gone silent
So I must decide.
This flesh is not mine
This skin is what's needed
Taken from one newly killed in the fray.
These Christian fools
Think I come as a reaper
A skeleton like the millions they bury.

Did you know that their amour grease is fat from their corpses?

With this disguise I'll find the answer.
To work then, to battle – I'll take on this madness.

History records how these nations failed you
Their rise and their fall are paved with your bodies
The line between murder and honour is fine
Today a medal – tomorrow a noose.

The sound of bullets becomes the sound of typewriter keys being depressed or an old-fashioned printing press running as we enter the office of GASTON CALMETTE.

SCENE 1
THE MADNESS OF MURDER
Paris, office of the Editor-in-Chief of Le Figaro
16 March 1914

A gloomy afternoon in the spacious office of the editor-in-chief of Le Figaro, a leading conservative newspaper. The desk is lit only by the light of a large brass banker's lamp with a green glass shade. GASTON CALMETTE is the Editor-in-Chief possibly because he is the son-in-law of the chairman of the board. He sits at the desk writing, dipping his pen into the ink bottle. The tall brass-handled double doors swing open.

CLERK: Excuse-moi, Monsieur Calmette…

CALMETTE: *(Without looking up from his manuscript, annoyed.)* I told you not to interrupt. I'm trying to prepare the editorial!

CLERK: *(Almost in a whisper.)* I'm sorry, Chief Editor. But it's Madame Minister of Finance Caillaux!

CALMETTE: *(Shocked.)* What – here?

MADAME HENRIETTE CAILLAUX enters. In no mind to wait until she is invited, she is already in the middle of the room. She is not only one of the most elegant, but also one of the most beautiful women in Paris.

She is dressed in grey and black and wears a thin veil. Her hat is large but still reveals her face and hair. She wears a muff, from which she will only remove her hand at the very end of the conversation. It is not as if she has come here to greet CALMETTE with a handshake.

CALMETTE bows deeply.

CALMETTE: Why, Madame, what an honour this is! A real pleasure!

HENRIETTE CAILLAUX: Always so cynical, Calmette. I very much doubt it's a pleasure.

CALMETTE gestures to two armchairs set apart downstage. As yet, he has not dared to sit down.

CALMETTE: My dear lady, why would I be cynical? My personal regard for you…

HENRIETTE CAILLAUX: …didn't stop you from stealing letters from me like a common thief – my letters to the Premier before he married me and –

She sits down.

CALMETTE: *(Hand on heart.)* Madame! Have I ever published anything by your fair hand?

HENRIETTE CAILLAUX: Not yet maybe – but tomorrow, next week, I'm sure you will. In any case, it makes no difference who they are from, mine to him or his to me. They are private letters, written when we were both married to other people. That does make a difference!

CALMETTE: I must say I'm shocked, Madame. You are calling me a common thief.

HENRIETTE CAILLAUX: No one believes you had the courage to break and enter yourself, of course. You have your minions for that – just as you are a minion to the English, those people who would have my husband removed from the office of Minister of Finance. They've already removed him from the Premiership – simply because he didn't want a war.

CALMETTE: Well, you see, Madame, we are faced with the threat of an encroaching German military operation. So it's hard to understand quite why your husband wants to get rid of our three-year conscription policy. I had the honour of being present when the King of Belgium informed our Premier of Germany's plan to invade France via Belgium if they did not dissolve their treaties with London…

HENRIETTE CAILLAUX: Monsieur Calmette, have you ever thought how the Germans must feel, knowing that our alliance with Russia was followed by other alliances with Italy and England? What kind of animal allows itself to be backed into a corner like that?

CALMETTE: The English treaty is purely defensive, a consequence of the speed at which the Kaiser is building a fleet. He poses a fatal threat to England. I can't believe that your husband can, as a Frenchman, be representing German interests…

HENRIETTE CAILLAUX: Monsieur, you are being stupid! You know very well that my husband saved world peace at Agadir. He brokered the deal with Berlin over the Congo. What was he to do? Allow our troops be butchered for the sake of the Congo?

CALMETTE: Madame knows as well as I that it was not about the Congo – it was about getting back Alsace-Lorraine. After the Congo-deal I felt I had to campaign for your husband's removal from the office of Premier. I will continue to oppose him.

HENRIETTE CAILLAUX: *(Imploringly.)* Monsieur Calmette! Not with these letters, I beg you.

CALMETTE: Let's get it straight, Madame. Your husband may be Finance Minister, but he backs those who refuse to fight. It's a monstrous treason! I can't say that openly, of course, because I have informants to protect. But your husband doesn't think twice about promoting that Socialist, the one who has the sheer nerve to claim that French workers will never shoot Germans. He seems bent on making Monsieur Jaurès Foreign Secretary! If he became Prime Minister again, he'd soon turn his back on his class, just as he did with the inheritance tax...

HENRIETTE CAILLAUX: Which proves how much of a patriot he is! Why else would a millionaire introduce an inheritance tax he is also subject to paying?

CALMETTE: I have my views on why a man would betray the class he comes from, the people who elected him.

HENRIETTE CAILLAUX: The wealthy detest my husband. He was elected by those who know that the welfare of France depends on peace, on trade relations, not on a war in which our youth bleed to death in Russia and in England...

CALMETTE: Madame forgets that, if everything went according to your husband's wishes, France would, for the first time in its history, have a Socialist Foreign Secretary in Jean Jaurès. He'd not only be betraying his own class, the nation too! A Socialist in the Quai d'Orsay!

HENRIETTE CAILLAUX: Monsieur Calmette, fight what you see as harmful to France, by all means do so. But fight fairly at least! Don't undermine my husband with stolen love letters from foreign power.

CALMETTE: You have no proof that the English provided me with letters from your husband. It's quite absurd!

HENRIETTE CAILLAUX: Tell me, Monsieur Calmette, where does your money come from?

CALMETTE: *(Laughs loudly.)* An amusing question from someone whose husband is practically synonymous with the Stock Exchange...and with the Bank of France!

She has stood up, is approaching the door. He follows, she stops and turns.

HENRIETTE CAILLAUX: Monsieur Calmette, you have to promise me you will not publish the letters, otherwise I will be forced...

CALMETTE: Believe me, Madame, my intention is entirely selfless: the welfare of France. If your husband became Premier again, it would be a serious risk. And this time with a Socialist Foreign Secretary who wants to prevent the workers of France from shooting the workers of the Kaiser!

HENRIETTE CAILLAUX: If you publish that kind of thing…

CALMETTE: I shall, and more! The voters cling to your husband, and they cling even more to Jaurès. I shall print everything. Your husband will be a dead man, finished! Everyone fights with the weapons they have.

HENRIETTE CAILLAUX: *(Calmly.)* If everyone fights with the weapons they have, then I shall have to shoot you.

CALMETTE: *(A short laugh.)* You are going to what? Oh, no!

'No' takes the form of a scream, but there he is now, laid low on the carpet by three shots from a revolver.

HENRIETTE CAILLAUX doesn't look at the dying man. Her revolver is smoking a little; she puts it back into her muff, from which she has produced it.

HENRIETTE CAILLAUX: 'Your husband will be a dead man.'

Behind her, a SECRETARY from the outer office comes bursting through the doors.

She just stands there, unable to move for 20 seconds before going across to the dead man. She kneels in order to lift CALMETTE's head. His clothing is covered in blood – the shots have gone through his chest and his belly. Finally, realising that she is unable to help the man on the floor, the SECRETARY looks up at the beautiful, composed-looking woman, lifts her head and yells.

SECRETARY: Police! Police!

She runs off as if he is being pursued. Without daring to enter the room, two colleagues of the dead man stand in the doorway, none of whom dares address MADAME CAILLAUX. She looks through them with total equanimity. A weakness then seems to come over her, and she sits down.

Eventually, she produces some Eau de Cologne from a small handbag. One of the EDITORS steps into the room, takes off his jacket, rolls it up and puts it under CALMETTE's head.

SECRETARY: I'm calling the Ministry of Finance! No, I'll get the Minister!

EDITOR 2: *(Calling after.)* You'd better go and find him. We can't tell him this on the phone!

EDITOR 3 is looking into the room, reluctant to enter. Both EDITORS stare at the dead man.

EDITOR 2: He wanted to fire me yesterday, just because I told him a gentleman wouldn't print private letters.

EDITOR 3: Why tell him that? He wasn't a gentleman at all. Call his wife!

The two EDITORS disappear. DEATH appears. He is at a loss as to what to say.

DEATH: *(Quietly.)* Is he dead?

He doesn't wait for an answer.

DEATH: Was it you?

HENRIETTE CAILLAUX: Please don't touch me! Show some respect for a lady.

This strange statement hangs in the air.

EDITOR 2: *(Young, helpless, shy.)* What do you mean? Did he try to rape you?

HENRIETTE CAILLAUX: In a way, yes. Blackmail.

EDITOR 3: He did. He blackmailed her!

Silence. She hands them her gun.

EDITOR 2: Has no one called a doctor?

DEATH: Why a doctor for a corpse?

The Minister of Finance, JOSEPH CAILLAUX, enters quickly.

CAILLAUX: I am the Minister of Finance! Acknowledge me properly!

The EDITORS salute, somewhat intimidated.

EDITORS: *(Mumbling.)* I beg your pardon, Monsieur Minister.

CAILLAUX: Thank you. You may go. Where is the doctor?

EDITOR 3: Should be here right away, Excellency. And the ambulance.

CAILLAUX nods to him.

CAILLAUX: Please be good enough to leave me alone with my wife…and the body.

HENRIETTE's hand searches for CAILLAUX's. He takes it.

Don't you think you rather overdid it, Henriette!

HENRIETTE: No. I love you, darling…and he wanted to kill you. He assured me he would never rest until you were – in his words – a dead man.

CAILLAUX: *(Shaken.)* I see. Well, he's dead now, our Monsieur Calmette. But so am I, Henriette. So am I.

SONG OF THE SCYTHES

DEATH: *(Turns to us and sings.)* Sssssssssssssh.
Can you hear
Can you hear
From far far away
The sound of the cutting machine
Line the road, fill the fields
With the bones of the dead
It's coming it's coming
To cut off your head

Not a pulse
Not a pulse
In the wrist of this cog
He's the first to fall under the blades
Clearing the path
For the great rows of teeth
That will slice you and dice you to death

He picks up CALMETTE and animates, dances with him.

Let us dance
Let us dance
On the ashes of life
Let us drink let us laugh let us sing

He goes to HENRIETTE CAILLAUX, who is sitting, motionless in the chair and gets her involved as –

Vive la France lady fair
She loves scandal today
Your noise will drown out the approach of the blades

While they gawp
At your plight
It will come to devour
And Calmette will have his way

The war they are winning
Will leave you all swimming
In the blood of the nine million dead

So climb on board
Climb on board
The cutting machine
Come along
Come along
For the ride
See it maim
See it kill
See it litter the roads
With the blood
Of all those who have died

Here it comes
Here it comes

(Spoken in tune.) Come on – jump on aboard
Never look right or look left
Satisfy your bloodlust

(Spoken – a pause in the music.) Come on now – come with us
In this glorious summer of death!

DEATH takes a prolonged applause and thanks the audience. He then announces:

DEATH: Danke schön meine Damen und Herren. Tonight's royal command performance in honour of His Imperial Majesty Franz Josef and his esteemed guest his Royal Highness King Edward the Seventh King of Great Britain and Ireland and Emperor of India for the auspicious occasion of this state visit of March 1909. Our evening's performance will recommence after this short interlude.

SCENE 2
KING EDWARD FAILS
Imperial Burgtheater, Vienna
March 1909

Anteroom leading to the Imperial box in the Viennese Burgtheater. We can see the box itself and as much of the audience and stage as possible. We hear the extended applause and audience murmurs as the first half of the gala performance comes to an end and the curtain falls.

His Imperial Highness EMPEROR FRANZ JOSEPH of Austria-Hungary, now 78 years old, has risen from his seat in the front row of the box and turns to his 67-year-old guest, KING EDWARD VII of Great Britain and Ireland and Emperor of India. As the applause continues, their two female companions stand up: the widowed Austrian PRINCESS STÉPHANIE and the British MRS ALICE KEPPEL, the wife of a naval officer and for many years now EDWARD's mistress.

They all politely suggest that each go first, exit the box and enter the anteroom.

A SERVANT enters and offers champagne.

FRANZ JOSEPH: *(As they toast each other.)* Well I must say I'm relieved that the play was your choice. Pretty cheeky really, portraying Downing Street like that. But you do have to laugh. Have you seen it before?

EDWARD: *(Laughs.)* The original production, about eight years ago!

ALICE KEPPEL: It was actually thirteen, sir: 1895!

EDWARD: *(Almost shocked.)* Good God, how time flies! He went to jail, you know, the playwright. Never wrote much after that. You can't see *An Ideal Husband* in London nowadays, so it's good to see it here. Poor Wilde! No more plays, I'm afraid. He died quite young, you know, after two years in prison.

STÉPHANIE: He went to jail because of *An Ideal Husband*, Uncle Bertie?

EDWARD: *(Laughs.)* Oh, no. It wasn't that. Pederasty in actual fact. Not the thing for a lady's ears.

FRANZ JOSEPH: Are you really that narrow-minded over there?

EDWARD: Well, it was also a question of…oh, what's the word?

EDWARD has forgotten the German word.

23

ALICE KEPPEL: I think you mean perjury, sir.

EDWARD: Thank you, yes: perjury. That's it.

He touches ALICE KEPPEL's arm.

EDWARD: The man perjured himself – rather honourably in fact. He had no wish to compromise another person.

EDWARD has taken a large cigar from the pocket of his uniform. One of the SERVANTS hurries to light the cigar as soon as he has used the cigar cutter. He smokes constantly and is rarely without an empty glass.

EDWARD: I take it you don't mind?

FRANZ JOSEPH: No, not at all. I quite like the smell.

ALICE KEPPEL gives a low curtsy. She has the most magnificent cleavage of all the women in the Burgtheater today, and EDWARD – who knows exactly what he wants to get from FRANZ JOSEPH – has instructed her to take away unnecessary listeners.

ALICE KEPPEL: *(With a low curtsy.)* Would you excuse me, your Majesty? I really would like to see your wonderful Hofburgtheater.

FRANZ JOSEPH: *(Helps her up. He rarely has the chance to view such a cleavage.)* By all means, Mrs Keppel. The archduchess will show you around. We feel honoured that you like what our architect has done with the place.

EDWARD: I attended the inauguration twenty years ago, you know.

FRANZ JOSEPH: Twenty-eight in fact. As you say, time flies!

STÉPHANIE: I'll gladly show you the building, Mrs Keppel, though I hardly know it. The inauguration was the last time I was here, with the Crown Prince…three months before his death.

EDWARD: *(He kisses her hand, with completely unfeigned sympathy.)* My dear Stéphanie – your poor Rudolf… *(This more to FRANZ JOSEPH.)* My eldest son too, you know.

FRANZ JOSEPH: *(In his presence his own son is never mentioned – an unwritten law, but not of course for the King of England.)* And mine, Kaiser Friedrich in Berlin! What a terrible time that was! People say the Burgtheater is the most beautiful thing built during my reign.

EDWARD: *(An accolade of the highest respect.)* Sixty years, sir. Quite incredible!

FRANZ JOSEPH: Even so, an unfortunate time to build it! Anyway, ladies, you need to hurry, or the intermission will be over.

ALICE KEPPEL curtsies again, as does PRINCESS STÉPHANIE.

EDWARD takes them to the door, and FRANZ JOSEPH signals for the SERVANTS to close both doors.

EDWARD: So here we are, just the two of us… About my brother-in-law, Kaiser Friedrich. When he died, I remember saying to my son, never forget Uncle Fritz, the most decent man I've ever known.

FRANZ JOSEPH: Indeed! I find it rather frightening. Why are we spared? Why are we allowed to reign for as long your mother reigned, when he had to die so quickly? A disaster too for your sister – Empress for a mere 99 days!

EDWARD: And to cap it all, such a difficult son!

FRANZ JOSEPH: I suppose so, yes. A mother's lot isn't an easy one.

EDWARD: On that subject, I don't like saying this about my nephew, but if that thing hadn't happened – I mean the problem with the boy's arm – Europe could sleep more soundly, I think. Wilhelm is so aggressive, has been…since childhood!

FRANZ JOSEPH: *(His tone different now, he assumes the demeanour of a ruler.)* My dear Edward, England has to understand, and they need to understand me too. December marks the 60th anniversary of my reign, you know. And when we annexed Bosnia and Herzegovina – 30 years ago now – Wilhelm gave us incredible support. So we could take that risk without fear of retribution from Russia!

EDWARD: Of course! Who cares if the Slavs kick up a fuss? Those two provinces were naturally yours. And by the way, since the Italians took territory from us and France in North Africa, we'd have no objection if you were to take back Northern Italy too. As for Russia, no Tsar will march against you without England's support! The only power that frightens the entire world now is Wilhelm…he's the one who'll drag you into war, and war is coming, mark my words! If he goes on building his fleet, I can't see any way out. Why, every one of his battle ships is now larger than England's.

FRANZ JOSEPH: I agree, it does have to stop, this mania for shipbuilding! But as you know, Edward, Wilhelm's ships do not threaten Austria.

EDWARD: On the contrary, they do. They threaten peace, which means you'll be drawn in. Your loyalty to Wilhelm will prove your undoing. Can't you see, Franz Joseph? You have to believe what I'm telling you. Have you forgotten that the Russians defended the Austro-Hungarian monarchy when you became King? As long as you don't side with the Germans against Russia, Russia will never march against you!

FRANZ JOSEPH: True enough, but the Germans have done nothing that would make me nullify our treaty. In fact, they've recently honoured it again in the face of a Serbian threat.

EDWARD: What about Sadová? They took that from you! And now Wilhelm's fleet, from which you'll reap no benefit, will bring us to the brink of war! And you'll be forced to honour your treaty with the Germans.

FRANZ JOSEPH: Sadová was 42 years ago. What's more, Bismarck could have humiliated us by marching on Vienna. But he didn't take a village from me, not even one!

EDWARD becomes cooler, for he sees – not for the first time – that this man is the only one in the world who cannot be made to waver in his loyalty to Wilhelm's Germany.

EDWARD: Wilhelm is not Bismarck. And even if Bismarck took nothing from you, he destroyed your two most loyal allies, swallowed them up completely: Hannover and Hesse. Did not the Lord Mayor of Frankfurt kill himself, when Bismarck…?

FRANZ JOSEPH: *(Annoyed.)* Yes, yes, you are right, of course… but the fact is I can always count on Berlin –

EDWARD: I'm sorry: no one can count on someone who instigates a global crisis every year…even if he's only blowing hot air. But in this case it's more than that. He's building a fleet intended to be stronger than ours; and he also has the largest army in the world!

FRANZ JOSEPH: He does not, Edward. Put Russia and France together, given their alliance, and the Germans are not half as strong!

EDWARD: But with your support...

FRANZ JOSEPH: *(Laughs.)* My dear Edward, I am seventy-eight years old! I've been on the throne for sixty years. You think I want a war at my age?

EDWARD: You may not start it, but Wilhelm will. And he knows you'll be with him! God knows what will happen to our people!

This measured expression of EDWARD's fear is paralleled by FRANZ JOSEPH's, but their conflict cannot be resolved.

FRANZ JOSEPH: *(Darkly.)* You seem not to want to understand, Edward. The more you paint this picture of Wilhelm, the more fearful I become of the thing you want me to do. If I break my treaty with Berlin – who can guarantee that they won't invade me as they did Maria Theresa 130 years ago?

EDWARD: You think we would allow Wilhelm to march on Austria?

FRANZ JOSEPH: You might not allow it but I doubt you could prevent it. Before the Russians could intervene, Wilhelm would have given Lemberg to the Tsar as a gift, perhaps even all of Austria-Poland; and Trieste would go to the Italians...and without Russia, France couldn't come to Austria's aid...wouldn't be able to!

EDWARD: *(Visibly hurt.)* So you really believe I'd hold back if Wilhelm...

FRANZ JOSEPH: My dear Edward, I believe the Germans would feel entitled to act against us simply to prevent us from joining the conspiracy you have in mind! So I can't consider it. That's all I have to say!

He suddenly stands up, goes to the door, knocks to have it opened.

FRANZ JOSEPH: Let's get back to *The Ideal Husband.*

EDWARD: *(Coldly – this rejected 'marriage proposal' is the only defeat he has ever suffered.)* Very well, though there is no conspiracy – merely a defensive alliance prompted by fear of Wilhelm. We don't expect you to march against Berlin; just not to march with him!

FRANZ JOSEPH makes an effort to calm himself, because the doors are now open. A SERVANT offers champagne. STÉPHANIE enters, without ALICE KEPPEL, looks at herself in a large mirror and busies herself with her hair.

FRANZ JOSEPH: I believe you when you call it defensive. But it simply isn't that anymore, not when four stand against one, which is what you are suggesting. They are odds which do not so much keep the one in check as force him to act. Better three against two. It's more likely to keep the peace.

EDWARD: *(Stubs his cigar out in a gesture of finality.)* Normally I agree. But he isn't normal.

FRANZ JOSEPH: He poses a danger, true enough, but more to me than to you!

EDWARD: *(To PRINCESS STÉPHANIE.)* My dear Stéphanie, ask the Emperor if he would allow you to visit us in Sandringham.

FRANZ JOSEPH: *(Before she can say thank you.)* But how could I refuse? By the way, I've never been to England myself!

EDWARD: My dear friend, London would receive you with open arms. Please come soon!

FRANZ JOSEPH: *(He knows how meaningless this offer is.)* Thank you, yes. We have to arrange it!

EDWARD exits quickly to relieve himself before the performance resumes.

FRANZ JOSEPH: *(Keeping an eye on the door.)* You seem rather sad, my dear Stéphanie.

STÉPHANIE advances towards the box's balustrade and looks down into the stalls through a gap in the curtain.

STÉPHANIE: This theatre, your Majesty…Marie Vetsera sat there during the inauguration…in the box in the middle gallery, second seat from the left. Rudolf only had eyes for her, but I had no idea…well, you know… But you are sad too, your Majesty.

FRANZ JOSEPH: *(Quietly.)* Well, Edward never brings us any luck! But I wonder if this time he might just be right. *(Fiercely, after he has glanced towards the door and convinced himself that they are not being overheard.)* He brought Vetsera and Rudolf together, you know.

STÉPHANIE: What? I don't understand. How could he have known her?

FRANZ JOSEPH: Through one of her people. He raced his horses against Bertie's.

EDWARD: *(Returning with ALICE KEPPEL.)* Your staircase is a pure symphony – marble transformed into melody.

ALICE KEPPEL: Your Majesty, it must be the most beautiful theatre in the world! The Parisian opera house is simply showy compared to this. *(To EDWARD.)* Why did this Mr Semper never design anything for you?

EDWARD: *(Smiling, a dull attempt to hide his almost paralyzing disappointment.)* You should ask his Majesty. It's perfectly clear to me why he didn't want to lend me his architect!

ALICE KEPPEL: To tell you the truth, I have never seen a more majestic staircase!

FRANZ JOSEPH: *(Still not in the mood for small talk again, bows.)* Madame is far too kind. The British can appreciate all this, but the Viennese are never satisfied. They say that in the new opera house they can't hear anything, in the new parliament building they can't see anything – and here in the Burgtheater they can neither see nor hear.

ALICE KEPPEL: I heard everything perfectly in the opera house, just perfectly. And here…

FRANZ JOSEPH: Well, the opera house does have its faults. The building is too low and dark, like some sort of Oriental caravan park. Unfortunately, I told the architect what I thought. I shouldn't have done so. He went and killed himself! Anyway, back to the play. Ladies!

The lights change, and the KAISER's Waltz begins to play.

EDWARD: Text from England, music from Vienna: what a perfect combination!

THE LEMMING SONG

DEATH enters. He is smiling an odd fixed smile. He begins to march manically on the spot in time to the music.

DEATH: What is this animal bloodlus
    That rages so through me?
    A fire in the bloodstream
    That makes me want to punch

So this is what it means
So this is what it means
So this is what it means to be you!

Lemmings
Lemmings
Walk right off the cliff
Into the waiting arms of death
Into the Abyss

Lemmings
Lemmings
Your madness makes me scream
You desire the blood of war
And what's worse is that you see

Lemmings
Lemmings
Who inflicts this doom?
Is it God? No it's you his little creatures
Killing in the gloom

As this chorus goes on it becomes more and more of a scream.

Lemmings
Lemmings
Your machines real speed things up
More blood, more fire, more pain more kill
More screaming from the holes and hills
More horror, madness, blinding pain
More souls come screaming down like rain
More stench more empty eyeless corpse
More murder gowned as rictus war
More rats, more lice more trenches deep
More wire more pyres more corpses reek
More stiff with rigor's blackened mask
More executions on the grass
More torture, darkness, no-man's-land
More gaping wounds more surgeon's hands
More disembowelling bayonet's tip
More gas more fire more stomachs ripped
More terror, white-eyed shaking goons

More poignant poems from Sassoon
More bombs more guns more snipers snares
More madness madness everywhere
More madness madness everywhere
More madness madness everywhere!

So this is what it means
This is what it means
This is what it means to be you!

SCENE 3
HIS MAJESTY'S MASTER SPY
The Reich Chancellery, Berlin
May 1914

DEATH produces a document. He says to the audience:

DEATH: The Reichskanzlei Berlin May 1914. And Chancellor
Theobald Bethmann-Hollweg is deeply concerned about
the document he has received from the Reich's most
important spy: it proves what the British Foreign Minister
Sir Edward Grey still officially denies: namely, that the
'talks' that have been going on for the last ten years
between Paris, London and Petersburg and which Britain
declares to be 'military consultations' have resulted in
contracts of alliance.

*Foreign secretary, GOTTLIEB VON JAGOW has just received the
documents and brought them directly to his comrade.*

*The two men enter the palatial office from the grand terrace and
remove their top hats.*

DEATH, a servant, is exiting. BETHMANN calls after him.

BETHMANN: Show Dr Wolff in at once. No one else – the
Editor-in-Chief only!

SERVANT: Yes, Mr Chancellor.

SERVANT exits.

BETHMANN: No, no, my dear Jagow, we cannot inform the
Kaiser! He talks too much. I've never heard anyone sober
talk as much as he does. Care for a cigar?

JAGOW sits.

31

JAGOW: *(Curtly.)* Thank you, no. I've given up smoking... I must say, Excellency, this is the most serious document we've received, ever since Bismarck obtained the Parisian declaration of war – and you don't want to show it to his Majesty?

BETHMANN: Not even to the Chief of Staff. Well, of course I shall inform Moltke, but only in broad, general terms. Dr Wolff similarly. This spy of ours is worth entire battalions. We can't afford to put him at risk.

BETHMANN cuts a cigar and smokes it, still standing with his hat on, while JAGOW has taken his top hat off. He removes his gloves and unbuttons his coat.

JAGOW: If only I could meet this spy!

BETHMANN: He works for us without payment, you know!

JAGOW: I could meet him in London, just for a drink and a chat, set aside my suspicions, make sure he is what we think he is.

BETHMANN: Don't be ridiculous, Jagow! Every word he's delivered confirms our suspicions. He doesn't create new fears, he merely confirms that we aren't paranoid, that all three are actually plotting against us.

JAGOW: I see. But I still find it strange that the Russians employ a Baltic noble with a German mother and a German name – Siebert – in their London embassy, and as their second secretary? And his brother is married to a German too!

BETHMANN: It does seem odd, I agree.

JAGOW: Then again, it seems they allow this Siebert to work at night for as long as he wants...

BETHMANN: There are such people in every office, Jagow... but it's not as if he's copying documents for us every evening! It won't arouse suspicion.

JAGOW: Perhaps not. I assume that, as second secretary, he has a key to the safe behind the ambassador's desk. Anyway, this document...how long do you think he took to copy it? He could hardly do so in twenty minutes!

JAGOW takes a paper from the folder; a translation of the document copied from classified documents and turned over to the Germans.

In any case, I agree that Theodor Wolff shouldn't see what we've received. Just tell him that the information reached us from Paris by means of a conversation.

BETHMANN: You think that enough to suggest its seriousness? Of course I won't mention London!

JAGOW: A conversation of an official nature, of course. But I still worry about the way in which the document came to us. It seems too simple...the fact that this Siebert actually writes to us...

BETHMANN: You could, my dear fellow, get used to not saying his name so often...

JAGOW: But it's unbelievable! He reveals his name to us when the papers would have been sufficient! And it seems he takes a hansom cab, a run-of-the-mill hansom cab, from the Russian to the German embassy. And he doesn't think the coachman might think it suspicious, driving from the Tsar's embassy to the Kaiser's in the middle of the night... Unbelievable, Excellency! Unbelievable!

BETHMANN: Yes, it is rather risky, but then...we aren't natural spies.

JAGOW: Well then, might I respectfully suggest that he should at the very least deliver the papers somewhere else...

SERVANT opens the door on the right. JAGOW has already put the folder into a desk drawer.

SERVANT: Mr Editor-in-Chief Dr Wolff!

BETHMANN warmly greets the man he has summoned here. DR THEODOR WOLFF bows in the doorway, leaving his cane and straw hat to the SERVANT. Handshake.

BETHMANN: My dear Dr Wolff! Thank you for coming so quickly.

WOLFF: *(To both.)* Excellency! It sounded quite dramatic!

JAGOW shakes the hand of the most famous journalist of the Reich, the Editor-in-Chief of the liberal Berliner Tageblatt.

JAGOW: I would have sent our coach, Doctor, but what the Chancellor is about to say is far too secret for you to be seen in it...

BETHMANN: Indeed! But I suggest that when you leave, you do so by the garden gate.

He indicates a seat, then sits down himself.

BETHMANN: You need to understand that no one must know that it was I or the Foreign Secretary, or anyone at all from these offices, who told you this. We leave it to your imagination, Dr Wolff, to inform your readers how you came about this information. Perhaps we could say it was in Paris.

WOLFF: *(Shrugs.)* I was there quite recently, in fact.

JAGOW: *(Still standing.)* I read your impressive eyewitness report – about the English King's State Visit.

WOLFF: On the 21st April.

BETHMANN: Barely four weeks ago. You could suggest you got wind of this on that occasion. *(With deep dismay.)* You are going to find this hard to believe, my friend. War is about to be declared. The only thing missing is the date! But once they put a date to it, the Russians and the French will descend on us. And what is that date? I suggest the day when England decides to join them.

WOLFF: I'd say that's impossible, if your Excellency weren't saying exactly what Colonel House told the German Ambassador in Washington. As you know, the American President himself sent House to Europe…

JAGOW: I know, House visited me.

WOLFF: And if he's telling the German ambassador that the three of them will invade us as soon as England says yes…

BETHMANN: They have said yes! We have it in writing. They are already exchanging details with the Russians of how British ships will provide cover for the Russians when they land. And we already know that almost 200,000 British troops will assist French armies on the right flank…

WOLFF: As a culmination of the agreements between the French and British armies since 1904! Which means that they would intercept the German advance through Belgium. I'll be frank, Excellency. Are you quite sure that England would involve itself at all if the Reich had another strategy that didn't use Belgium as an access point to Paris? After all, England has always allied itself with the Netherlands and Belgium.

BETHMANN: *(Helplessly.)* The General Staff assures me that France cannot be attacked head-on, on account of its forts...

WOLFF: *(Unsure.)* But, Excellency, these forts are surely an indication that France wants to stay on the defensive? The Russians have no such fortresses because their intention is to invade us. But why should Germany invade France, if the French only want to stay in their fortresses?

BETHMANN: *(Impatient.)* Dr Wolff, I am not a strategist, I am...the Chancellor. The details of the battlefield...

WOLFF: Excuse me, Excellency. Plans that include neutral neighbours like Belgium, are no longer details of the battlefield. They are political! Cannot the Chancellor inform the General Staff which borders he...

JAGOW smiles to himself, he agrees with WOLFF but does not dare say this to BETHMANN's face. He also secretly agrees with WOLFF.

BETHMANN: I'm afraid not, Wolff. But if you, as representative of the most important Berliner newspaper, and as someone not directly affiliated to the government, wish to serve your country...

WOLFF: *(Somewhat hurt.)* 'Wish to'? What else would I want but to serve the Fatherland?

BETHMANN: *(Puts a hand on his arm.)* Of course! You wouldn't be here if we expected anything less. Anyway, I have seen documents, actually seen them – but that's for you alone to know! To your readers you have to say that a person on the inside of the entente confirms that this summer, Petersburg and London are working out a Russian-British naval strategy. Ask the question in the Tageblatt: what does London have against the Reich? This report confirms once and for all that, without a strong German fleet, the Reich will be exposed to a Russian invasion with the assistance of British ships. And ask as well how these naval plans fit in with the assurances from the British Foreign Office...

JAGOW: *(Interjecting.)* If I may, Excellency, I suggest that Dr Wolff does not speak in general terms of the Foreign Office, but that he refer specifically to their Foreign Secretary Sir Edward Grey…that will force him to address Parliament as soon as the British papers start quoting claims made in the Berliner Tageblatt.

BETHMANN: An excellent idea, Jagow. Sir Edward has so often assured us there is no alliance. So he is bound to speak if he is directly involved.

WOLFF: I must say you flatter a newsman, gentlemen. The Chancellor of the German Reich trusts the press to be able to force England's Foreign Minister to divulge publicly one of his best-kept secrets! Amazing! But what if Grey remains silent? What if he fails to oblige us with an answer? Can you then reveal your informant?

BETHMANN: *(Shocked.)* I'm afraid not! But between us we can – in a way, I don't yet quite know how – ensure that Grey does not get away with it.

He rings, and the SERVANT enters.

BETHMANN accompanies WOLFF to the terrace. JAGOW shakes hands with the editor. BETHMANN speaks to the SERVANT.

BETHMANN: Show Dr Wolff to the garden gate. And thank you, Doctor.

SERVANT: Yes, Chancellor.

The SERVANT brings WOLFF's stick and hat.

WOLFF: Excellency, I appreciate your faith in me. A newspaper may not be able to shoot, but I think it can help!

JAGOW: I imagine your colleagues in England, and in Paris too no doubt, will make a fuss when they realise the threat posed by the ever-peaceful Russians and British.

WOLFF bows and exits. BETHMANN waves after him. Very different now, totally dismayed he says to JAGOW:

BETHMANN: England wasn't even part of the anti-Prussian coalition, and today it is! Russia was still distant, but today it is on top of us, right by the Alps. They edge ever closer via the railroads… Every time I plant a tree on my Estate, I ask myself: does it matter anymore? Jagow! Have you seen a map recently? Soon the Russians will be sitting in the shade of the trees I plant!

BETHMANN wipes his forehead with a handkerchief; JAGOW raises both hands, as if help could come 'from above'…

THE ESPIONAGE SONG

DEATH: *(Sings.)* Of course I'm not for the war
 It limits my freedom to trade
 But even at that,
 If you're smart with your cash
 You can rake in the money in spades.

 Now if they so much as sniffed
 That when I go trading abroad,
 The enemy pays up
 For tales that I dig up
 About our troop movements at home

 Before the bloody war,
 All my bets were on
 Now you're a traitor
 Just 'cause you make a
 Dollar or two of your own!

 Why shouldn't I sell some secrets
 To all those who want to pay?
 So my wealth I disguise
 And I have alibis
 So the government think I obey

 The press, the people the state
 They'd drag my name through the mud.
 But if they find money
 I'll say What? That's funny!
 Now where's the proof, m'Lud?

 I have contacts spread far and wide
 Based in countries who're out of the war

That funnel the money
That might be called funny
Back to this naughty old whore

So I'm up for sale today!
Who wants to put on a bid?
You can have what you like
If the money is right
Pay up and the secrets are yours
You can have what you like
If the money is right
Pay up and the secrets are yours.

SCENE 4
CHURCHILL'S BAIT
The Deck of the RMS Lusitania
March 1914

There is the sound that sets the scene – the low hum of ship's horns. DEATH is now an officer.

DEATH: The deck of the RMS Lusitania. March 1914.

He turns as WINSTON S. CHURCHILL and LORD ALFRED BOOTH enter.

CHURCHILL (now only 39) is the First Lord of the Admiralty. He speaks in a rough, very fast, sometimes lisping, but always cultivated manner. BOOTH (almost ten years his junior) wears a bowler hat and, later, an expensive fur-lined black coat. He too is the lord of a powerful realm, namely the Cunard-Line, but listens to the young minister like a trained dog, meek, eager and overwhelmed. In this case it is not just the aura of power that intimidates BOOTH, but the sheer volume of talk in which CHURCHILL indulges.

DEATH: Lord Booth, Lord Churchill.

DEATH exits.

CHURCHILL: I wanted to speak to you alone, Mr Booth. You see, they now insist on keeping minutes at the Admiralty.

He looks at BOOTH with the amusement of a man who, thanks to his own historical knowledge, always sees himself making history.

CHURCHILL: I hope you don't keep a diary.

BOOTH: *(Solicitous.)* No, Mr Churchill, I do not, but perhaps I should if what you announced last week is true: war with Germany, maybe in September.

CHURCHILL: Did I say 'maybe'? I should have said definitely! We will definitely be at war in September... But in any case, I regard myself more as a writer than a Minister. I've always earned my living with the pen. Hence my advice, Mr Booth – never keep a diary!

BOOTH tries to conceal how shocked he is that CHURCHILL can speak of war as if it were the weather.

BOOTH: I find it hard to believe that you, Minister, can, after 40 years of peace in Europe, speak so lightly of a British-German conflict...

CHURCHILL: *(Interrupts him almost angrily.)* Never lightly, my friend. For the last eighteen years, ever since the Kaiser appointed Tirpitz to the Admiralty, it has been the goal of those two men to 'out-build' us, as Tirpitz recently admitted in Berlin. Why is it that the Hun kicks us in the stomach when we hold out our hand to them? Ever since our War Minister was sent packing from Berlin last year without an explanation, he is convinced that we have to fight. The question is, how do we get the Germans to fire the first shot? Democracies demand that you hold back until the other person reveals his hand.

BOOTH: *(Sceptically amused.)* Will the Germans be stupid enough to shoot first?

CHURCHILL: They won't fire on us, of course. But we should heed Bismarck's warning: the only place where a war could start would be in the Balkans. My parents went on visiting Bismarck after he was forced out, you know.

Enter LADY JENNIE RANDOLPH.

My mother can tell you all about it! Mama, may I introduce you to the owner of the Lusitania, Mr Booth...

BOOTH: *(Laughs, says quickly.)* Nonsense, Mr Churchill, I'm a mere shareholder, like thousands of others.

Bowing, he removes his bowler hat and walks quickly past CHURCHILL, forcing him to step back. He approaches LADY

RANDOLPH, who moves towards the two men with light, swift steps. Now this beautiful woman holds out a hand to BOOTH and addresses him with a laugh.

LADY RANDOLPH: Why, Mr Booth, I've sailed on many liners, but none as beautiful a boat as this.

BOOTH: Then you should return to New York with us, Lady Randolph.

LADY RANDOLPH: I'm afraid not. Winston's about to be a father again. My daughter-in-law needs me, so we disembark at Liverpool. But another time, of course I'll be glad to sail on the Lusitania.

BOOTH: Mr Churchill thinks we shall be at war quite soon. Don't you share his pessimism?

LADY RANDOLPH: *(She affectionately grabs her son by the lapels.)* Oh, Winston's always talked of war, ever since he was capable of speech. Look at his books: eight volumes in eight years – and only his father's biography not about war! Still, my sister-in-law. Daisy Pless – she thinks she's the only woman to love the Kaiser, you know – she assures me that Wilhelm is running scared.

CHURCHILL: *(Darkly.)* Scared? I think his generals might think him scared. So now he has to demonstrate that even a one-armed man can shoot.

LADY RANDOLPH: *(Vivacious.)* Anyway, what's all that to do with the biggest and fastest passenger ship in the whole world? As for the rest, Winston, I'm sure you have the strongest fleet to stop the Germans from showing up in the Atlantic…if there's a war, that is.

CHURCHILL: *(Gruffly.)* Have you never heard of a submarine, Mama!

LADY RANDOLPH: *(Sarcastically.)* I've never heard of submarines attacking passenger ships, and neither have you! Tell me, Mr Booth, how fast is the Lusitania?

BOOTH: Twenty-four knots, Lady Randolph.

LADY RANDOLPH: *(To CHURCHILL.)* And German submarines, Winston?

CHURCHILL: *(As sarcastically as she spoke to him.)* Much slower, I admit. *(Impatiently.)* But we shouldn't be keeping Mr Booth. He wishes to make a telephone call!

BOOTH: That's right, Lady Randolph. You'll have to excuse me. I neglected to tell my agents that the press aren't to know you are both on board.

LADY RANDOLPH: *(Surprised.)* But why? You should have told me, Winston. I'd have stopped them taking my picture when we came on board.

BOOTH: *(Doffing his hat, bowing.)* Well at least they didn't take a shot of Mr Churchill. Goodbye, Lady Randolph. I'll see you at lunch. Mr Churchill promised you'd tell me about Bismarck!

LADY RANDOLPH: Sure, if you're interested…see you soon!

BOOTH exits. LADY RANDOLPH links arms with her son, they walk along the deck.

I'm curious, Winston. Why shouldn't the papers know we're on the Lusitania?

CHURCHILL: As you know, Mama, we have the Admiralty yacht for ordinary cruising. If it's known that I'm on the Lusitania, they'll want to know why.

LADY RANDOLPH: So why are you?

CHURCHILL: Because last week I issued an order…that this and 39 other passenger and merchant ships be equipped with weapons by next spring.

LADY RANDOLPH: *(Astonished.)* But why, Winston, would you want war?

CHURCHILL: We cannot wait for the Kaiser to decide whether or not I'm still allowed to take a walk on the deck of this ship with my mother.

LADY RANDOLPH: *(Outraged.)* Is this some sort of joke? How on earth can the Kaiser determine that?

CHURCHILL: It's far from a joke, Mama. Despite the fact that the Franco-Russian alliance threatens him on land, he goes on building ships. And for what purpose? To attack us, of course! This fleet is the brainchild of German irrationalism. And we have to stop irrational people before they run amok.

LADY RANDOLPH: I seem to recall you telling the House quite recently that by next year we would have ten more battleships, each of them twice as powerful as any enemy ship. So why turn the Lusitania into a cruiser?

CHURCHILL: I shall use the Lusitania as bait, all 45,000 tons of her!

LADY RANDOLPH: Really, Winston! Does the gunsmith ever ride into battle? I've never heard of it. So why would America want to join the fight? It's making a fortune from the sale of arms.

CHURCHILL: We could well need America to save us. But since there is no guarantee that Germany will attack the USA, the American public must be roused, outraged, if they are to become involved. And the sinking of a ship carrying American civilians would easily achieve that. *(Angry at his mother.)* Mama, why look at me like that? We do this for England, not for personal profit!

LADY RANDOLPH: Winston, it's not because I'm American. It's because you are so unscrupulous!

CHURCHILL: It's nothing to do with scruples! If the USA were to join us, the Germans would have second thoughts.

LADY RANDOLPH: Then you have to make sure the Americans know, before they are called up.

CHURCHILL: I think not. No president could ever guarantee me that. If we were to offer France or Russia unconditional support, they'd have us in their pocket. They'd be marching on Berlin before we knew it. Such promises become a binding contract... Ah, Booth!

BOOTH: *(Already calling out before we see him. He enters without coat or hat.)* Just heard on the wireless, Paris in a state of panic. The Finance Minister's wife...she's shot the editor of Le Figaro...in his office apparently!

CHURCHILL is beaming. His mother puts her hand to her mouth in horror.

LADY RANDOLPH: Madame Caillaux? For heaven's sake, why?

CHURCHILL: Why? If one's offered a gift-horse, why ask why? Caillaux's out of the picture! That's good enough for me!

BOOTH: Surely, Minister, it's the editor who's out of the picture.

CHURCHILL: Mr Booth! They are both out of the picture. Caillaux was a markets man, never keen on war, rather like our Lloyd George. Weapons manufacturers want war, traders and merchants want peace.

LADY RANDOLPH: But why did his wife shoot the editor? Why?

CHURCHILL: He intended to publish the letters that she and Caillaux wrote to each other while they were married to other people. As a matter of fact, we leaked them to Calmette… As they say, a woman wronged!

LADY RANDOLPH: Women, Winston, react to what is done to them, and rightly so!

CHURCHILL: *(Laughs.)* I can't think why she had to shoot him dead! Rather drastic, don't you think?

LADY RANDOLPH: *(Very matter-of-fact.)* Things never go to plan, in love or war. Women can teach you a few things, Winston. Men may hit, women hit back!

CHURCHILL: I need a drink!

THE BLOOD PUMP

Enter a WOMAN, a war widow. She is now a seamstress in her uniform of apron and armband, and carries a pincushion. A sad, withered face and a shy manner.

She takes the dust sheet off a Prussian general's uniform and, in the way that seamstresses do, busies herself with chalk in front of a mannequin. The military uniform is studded with decorations, from the spiked helmet to the spurred leather boots, which, together with the sabre and the black-and-white sash, dangle and flap whenever she turns or moves the mannequin. The general's white gloves are placed under the left epaulet.

DEATH enters quickly, not in uniform but as the skeleton, wearing his black cowl, which he later throws aside.

WOMAN: Your uniform is ready.

DEATH: You think I'll wear that?
    Not in a thousand years!
    The worst butcher's outfit?
    I won't dress like Falkenhayn
    I'm no general, no madman.

WOMAN: Falkenhayn is the chief of staff.

How dare you talk of him this way.
You should be honoured to wear this
Glorious cloth

DEATH: I'm not that butcher and never will be
A criminal mind who hates humanity.
He coined the phrase 'bleed the enemy white'
Did you know that?
He bled them white alright
And his own troops
Bled them until the rivers ran red.
His blood pump. Verdun.
The earth's artery
The blood of one million eight hundred
Haemorrhaging into the soil.
Verdun.
A deadly maw
Feeding troops in
To the cutting machine
The human meat grinder
And you
Want me, to put this on?
I'm not the kind of pig
Who devours his piglets

WOMAN: The war in the West must be won.

DEATH: The 'strategy'
He called it, our German Chief of Staff
Erich Falkenhayn the 'great man'

WOMAN: This is our duty unto the last

DEATH: It's not me you're dressing.
You're dressing him,
He who lays the longest row of graves
Endless stretching soldiers fallen.
This murderer's costume…
I'll have none.

WOMAN: Do you think that we sacrificed our
Loved ones, our best, our sons,
So you could refuse to play your part?

DEATH: Your husband was killed – when?

Where, in which battle?
I'm not in touch anymore!
You look at me
As if it's my fault he died
By flamethrower, was it?
But burning soldiers alive
Has never been my style.

Killing today has no sex appeal.
Oh, for God's sake, stop crying!
It was already too much for me
In the first year of war.
I release soldiers from their fear of death,
I snuff the screaming of the maimed.

WOMAN: We dress them in khaki
Send them to fight
And yet, here you are
Refusing the call.
Then a coward is what you are
Nothing more.

She hands him a white feather.

DEATH takes the feather. He is clearly in conflict – he clutches it as woman exits. Then –

DEATH: Wait! Come back.
I'm a coward that's true
But better a coward than a butcher
I'll put it on – but – just for a minute
Understand that's all it will be
A minute. A minute will help me see –

He puts on the uniform. He starts talking in a military fashion. His posture changes.

One million eight hundred thousand soldiers,
Eliminate them here.
Here in this place
Wear them down,
Accept the strategy, overrun Verdun!
Germany could not take Verdun quickly,
As his Excellency explained to the Kaiser,

The French would not have come to defend it.
Now they are there. 'Bleed them white', says the general.
Our troops will suffer too,
But the number of the enemy killed
Will be greater still; they will use
More ammunition, more guns.
The Reich must use the time well,
For if it does not take Paris
Before the Americans march into France,
The Kaiser could lose the war...

He laughs, like Falkenhayn would laugh at the best joke in the Potsdam officer's mess. Then he continues.

Bleed them white that's the strategy.
One million eight hundred thousand men!
Die in one place! Die in Verdun!
Corpses piled so high they're blocking out the sun!
Endless death. Endless rivers of blood
The world before Auschwitz never witnessed
A steeper mountains of skulls.

As he is about to march off, he roots around in the pockets of his breeches until he finds his wallet. He finds some money, which the seamstress gratefully accepts. He then finds a note. He reads as the scene changes:

DEATH: 'You want to portray a murder? So show me the dog in the yard: at the same time show me the shadow of the deed in the eye of the dog'.

SCENE 5
SHOTS IN SARAJEVO
A Viennese Cafe
28 June 1914

A typical 'Viennese' café, new in Sarajevo. The interior of the café, in Art Nouveau style, is intended to emphasize the loyalty of the owner to Vienna and the monarchy. One WAITER, no waitress. White-rimmed mirrors behind the wide, white, opulently laden buffet.

The WAITER goes over to a man who is sitting alone in a corner, at a round marble table with iron legs. DRAGUTIN DIMITRIJEVIĆ, a general from the Belgrade Secret Service known as the Black Hand, sits dressed as an Orthodox priest. He looks towards the buffet then the kitchen door but otherwise speaks quite unconcernedly for now the WAITER, as we can see through the window, is in front of the café. We can hear cheering which gets louder and louder until it drowns out the slowly fading national anthem of Austria 'God Save Emperor Francis'.

Sitting a little way apart is a nervous young cobbler, TRIFKO GRABEŽ. He is really a student pretending to be a Muslim cobbler. He wears a colourful fez. He is waiting for someone. From their tables they can see through the large windows which reach down to the pavement.

WAITER: The Archduke won't be driving past here, you know. That's why we've got no other customers. They're all watching the parade.

DIMITRIJEVIĆ: We are loyal Serbs, my friend. Why would we want to see an Austrian?

WAITER: *(Goes out into the street.)* I'm a Bosnian too, Father, but what's so wrong about wanting to see the Archduke? It's not exactly treason, is it? Don't mean I support him. Too many Serbs do that already.

DIMITRIJEVIĆ: We must be mad sitting here, drawing attention to ourselves.

GRABEŽ: Always wise after the event, Major.

DIMITRIJEVIĆ: Too late now. Here's the ice cream... This place. Look at it! Far too posh for a cobbler – even a pretend one! Your father wouldn't have been seen dead in it! We should have gone somewhere more suitable... though I should have known you're an intellectual, not a cobbler. I could tell by the way you walk.

GRABEŽ: *(Laughs.)* My grandmother used to say I was like my father in all sorts of ways.

DIMITRIJEVIĆ: *(In a better mood.)* Well, she was wrong. You can always tell what a person is by the way he walks. And you walk like a student.

GRABEŽ: Alright, maybe I do. Why so touchy?

DIMITRIJEVIĆ: I'm not. Just nervous. I'd rather be involved than sit here waiting.

GRABEŽ: So why are we waiting? I mean they all said they'd be taking the cyanide if they pulled it off or not.

DIMITRIJEVIĆ: I can't leave while they are still out there. God knows, they might be lynched on the spot if the cyanide doesn't work. Or their guns might jam, in which case they can come and get two more from us. I'm in favour of shooting, anyway. You throw a bomb, it might not go off, and someone throws it back at you. As for grenades, you throw them too early, they go off before they hit the target. No, give me a gun any day!

GRABEŽ: I'm told Princip got up early, 5 o'clock apparently, put a candle on Bogdan Žerajić's grave.

DIMITRIJEVIĆ: *(Angrily.)* He should have stayed in bed, made sure his hand's steady for the job. Why pay your respects to a hopeless failure? The only thing he got right was shooting himself. Five shots at the governor and they all missed. The only one that didn't was the sixth, the one he shot himself with. God forbid, what sort of person would even think of honouring the grave of such a loser? A bloody poet, that's who! Pathetic!

GRABEŽ: You think a poet can't be an assassin, Major? A famous German said as much: 'Today a poet, tomorrow a killer of kings!'

He smiles, speaks with dignity.

DIMITRIJEVIĆ: *(Laughing.)* Who was it said it?

GRABEŽ: A writer called Lessing, Major. A great writer.

DIMITRIJEVIĆ: Never heard of him. So the place where Princip lived...has it been cleared out?

GRABEŽ: Yes sir. Clothes, books, everything.

DIMITRIJEVIĆ: Wait there! Something's happened.

DIMITRIJEVIĆ gets up excitedly, pushing the boy back into the chair as he tries to get up.

Remembering that he is supposed to be a priest, he walks slowly in the direction of the door and goes out to the WAITER, who, unheard by us, is speaking to two passers-by. They too are colourfully dressed as Muslims. The WAITER wants to come back into the café to tell what he has heard, but the way is momentarily blocked by DIMITRIJEVIĆ. The passers-by have gone on.

WAITER: A bomb, sir. Half an hour ago. The Archduke's car! Seems it missed. Hit the car behind.

DIMITRIJEVIĆ: *(Masking his urgent curiosity.)* You mean the attempt failed? Heaven forbid! These foreigners lead charmed lives! What else did they say?

WAITER: The one who threw the bomb, he tried to escape, but they caught him.

GRABEŽ: *(Unable to hide his fear, his voice raised.)* They caught him? What then?

DIMITRIJEVIĆ: *(Giving him a crushing look.)* I assume they killed him on the spot.

WAITER: They got him on the Miljacka bridge. Seems the Archduke was bleeding furious. Left the town hall after ten minutes. Imagine! A State Visit ten minutes long!

DIMITRIJEVIĆ goes slowly downstage and sits down.

DIMITRIJEVIĆ: Probably out of Sarajevo by now. Can't think it's good for the city.

WAITER: No, sir. Seems he's still here. There's a big lunch in the Konak. Speaking of which, what can I get you gentlemen?

DIMITRIJEVIĆ: We'll have two double Slivovitz. We shall drink to his health. And the bill, please! *(To GRABEŽ. The WAITER has already gone to the buffet.)* For God's sake! What now?

GRABEŽ: Wasn't Čabrinović at the bridge?

DIMITRIJEVIĆ: Of course he was! He's a brave man, Čabrinović, no question of taking cyanide!

GRABEŽ: *(Fear welling up in him.)* Who knows! Maybe he didn't!

DIMITRIJEVIĆ gets his briefcase, checks the bill, pays the WAITER. The WAITER gives him change and takes the tip DIMITRIJEVIĆ pushes towards him.

WAITER: Thank you, thank you, Father.

DIMITRIJEVIĆ: Did they say what damage the bomb did?

WAITER: *(Shakes his head.)* A couple of people injured, that's all. Not the Archduke's car, though.

One can sense he is reluctant to serve a cobbler in this elegant café, so he makes a show of only speaking to the 'priest':

WAITER: Good thing the bomb didn't kill him. Wouldn't have done anyone any good, that… You know, he was in a bazaar last year…Mostar, I think, and this gypsy read his palm, said he'd start a big war, he'd be the cause of it… *(He tells this story animatedly.)* Anyway, Franz Ferdinand didn't believe a word of it. Just laughed, he did. Swore by the eyes of his three kids that he'd never do anything to the Serbs, wouldn't take a sheep or a single plum tree! He don't want no war, just to change things a bit. I don't know! That gypsy!

DIMITRIJEVIĆ: So you don't believe that superstitious nonsense?

WAITER: Course not, Father. The Archduke cause a war? He'll never do us any harm.

DIMITRIJEVIĆ: *(Happily.)* I very much doubt that he will. Thank you.

The 'thank you' is to shoo the WAITER away. DIMITRIJEVI raises his glass to GRABEŽ.

DIMITRIJEVIĆ: Here's to Princip!

GRABEŽ: To the liberation of Bosnia!

DIMITRIJEVIĆ: *(His face expresses deep disappointment, he murmurs more than speaks.)* Alright, no point in waiting any longer. The Archduke won't be coming this way again, not when he's greeted with bombs. He'll be out of here when it gets dark. No, you stay! Stick to the plan! Wait for your sister. Then you find your father. Tell him my shoe size is 24 and I'm coming to buy a pair of slippers. No need to take me via the smugglers' route again, my passport's fine, and since nothing's happened here…

GRABEŽ: How can you be so calm, Major? The longer you stay here, the greater the risk!

DIMITRIJEVIĆ: Not to worry, my friend. I feel quite safe as a priest. My passport guarantees it.

GRABEŽ: Before you go, Major, one more question. What the gypsy said…you think she's right?

DIMITRIJEVIĆ: Of course not! Franz Ferdinand will not be responsible for war, but he has to be removed. The Kaiser is 84. The Archduke will succeed him, and our dream of an independent Serbia will be over. He's a clever statesman. We will be bound to Austria, so we have to help him to meet his maker. Anyway, your sister's here. See what she has to say, then go! *(GRABEŽ remains seated instead of going out to the GIRL.)* She seems confused. Why doesn't she come in?

The GIRL is not yet visible to the audience. She has spotted a co-conspirator in the street. When she enters the café, we see she is veiled, like all Muslim women on the street. She is about 20 years old.

GIRL: It's really stupid this Muslim costume. Don't you know Muslims aren't allowed in cafés?

GRABEŽ: *(Irritated.)* Never mind that! Tell us what's happened!

The GIRL smiles, looks around. Because the WAITER is no longer there, she laughs aloud.

GIRL: We did it! Both of them dead! Both of them!

DIMITRIJEVIĆ: *(Whispering.)* What do you mean both? Who's dead?

GIRL: It was so easy. The car stopped in front of Princip. He couldn't miss.

DIMITRIJEVIĆ: Are you sure he's dead? That's not what we were told.

GIRL: The Archduke, yes. Like I said, he couldn't miss.

GRABEŽ: *(Whispering, trying not to shout.)* Stupid girl! What about Princip?

GIRL: He got hit on the head…with a sword. Covered in blood, he was. But he's not dead. They got hold of him. I heard him screaming for his life.

DIMITRIJEVIĆ: *(Mortified.)* What about the cyanide?

GIRL: I don't know. He was sick when they grabbed him…
maybe he'd swallowed it. If it wasn't for the police, they'd
have killed him.

DIMITRIJEVIĆ: *(Stops as he is about to go out.)* You say both
of them! God, the woman too! Why kill her? She's got
three children. We'll lose what sympathy we might have
gained… *(To GRABEŽ.)* Alright! You go to your father! *(To
the GIRL, giving her a large bill from his briefcase.)* You to the
Post Office. Telegraph Belgrade…your brother's landlord.
You've got the address?

GIRL: *(Impatiently.)* Yes, of course.

DIMITRIJEVIĆ: *(To GRABEŽ.)* Go on, then! And walk slowly!
(To the GIRL.) Send this message: 'Both horses sold'.

GIRL: Nothing else? Just that?

DIMITRIJEVIĆ: *(To the brother as well, who is still there.)* They'll
understand. Just tell your father I'll be there. He can take
me tonight, the same way as yesterday. Get your mother to
make up a bed. *(To the GIRL.)* OK. Send the message.

GIRL: *(Softly, happy, she goes out.)* Yes. 'Two horses sold'. Just
that!

DEATH AS A TEACHER

DEATH: Clatter clatter clatter
Down the drain
There goes peace
Man's beaten now
He's sealed his own fate.
He'll be reeling from the blow
Of the silver bullets
That killed the wolf
And brought down his fat lady wife.
For a long time to come
And here I am
Seasick
Aboard the Imperial Yacht
With the bloated
Self-important, appointed
Keepers of the people.

The very people
They're about to wipe out.
Oh look. Here he is
Grand Admiral Tirpitz.
Look – mighty Neptune's trident
Couldn't rival that beard
He's otherwise known as
The Father of lies – look at him
You can't trust him
To find you a life jacket
He loves his ships
His big boy's toys
He scares the people
Into hating England
So he can keep building up the fleet
He's lied to England's admirals
So he can surpass their might
But he doesn't want war.
He'll resist it and resist it because
It's safe to say
He's a coward, he's yellow
It's just about whose got
The biggest one –
If you know what I mean.

And here's that jackass Moltke
The German General chief of staff.
He's the armies leader
But only because his name
Is glorious and splendid
His uncle did the job
So the family stay connected
And he worked his way up
From great he slimed to greatest
Lubed by privilege and wealth
But he couldn't lead
A horse to water
Never mind run campaigns
He'll lose the war
For Germany

Underestimate the foe
Fail to control his armies
Because he's a frightened little soul
He's a tearful, cringing toady
He'll cry at the Kaiser's knee
But at least he'll understand
When Germany is beat.
For now he tells the Kaiser

MOLTKE: I'm not fit for the job.

DEATH: But the Kaiser won't listen.

KAISER: Don't panic.

DEATH: He says.

KAISER: You're fine for peace
And I'll lead in a war.

DEATH: And here's another suck up:
Stöwer the painting fool.
He does a good line in
Painting sinking ships
He'll be busy for a while.
And even when this is over
He'll talk of the glorious now,
Of the honour he felt
At witnessing these dunces
Sending millions to hell.

And the starring role
The Kaiser.
Such a puffed-up little man.
He is always right.
He's always the king.
He'll hear no dissent.
His ego's as big as a Zeppelin
It can block out the sun and the moon
He preens. He struts. Won't take advice.
Wouldn't know the truth
If it punched him and cried
I'm the truth! I'm the truth! You're a dolt!
You're insane!

His diplomacy is legend.
He hits Tsars at court
Humiliates kings
Calls emperors fools
And of his people –
He washes his hands
Daily in their blood.

Too much inbreeding, you might say,
Has produced
Little Caligula here
Too much blue blood
Mixed with blue blood
And not enough sacks to drown
Offspring at night
Look – he tightropes along a shady line
Between an insane and a disordered mind.
And all of them kowtow before him
Look at them fawn to their king.
So the scene is set
For this dance of death
The curtain rises on the end
Of what makes man good.
Watch them take away God.
Take away light
Watch them
Open the gates for the war horses.
The slaughtered
The innocent
The millions of corpses

Paint away, Kaiser. Paint away.
The forecast says it's a beautiful day.

SCENE 6
KAISERWEATHER
Deck of the Imperial SMY Hohenzollern
28 June 1914

DEATH takes a sea whistle out and blows on it as the scene is set, piping aboard TIRPITZ, the KAISER, MOLTKE, WEIZSÄCKER and STÖWER as they enter.

TIRPITZ's signature beard is styled in a manner like no one else fashioned it during this era: a short goatee under his chin, then two long beards on either side, not touching, that reach down to the bottom of the V of his jacket, ending in points. The 33-year-old ERNST WEIZSÄCKER, who had been in the navy since 1900, was often in the same room as the grand admiral.

The other men onboard the yacht are wearing the compulsory 'formal dress of the Imperial Yacht club': white on hot days but otherwise blue. The KAISER sits alone in a wide basket-chair, directly facing the railing. He is painting with watercolours, which he has an above-average talent for. The hand of the KAISER's withered left arm rests in his lap while his right hand paints. MOLTKE and WEIZSÄCKER are watching him paint from a respectful distance, but TIRPITZ has come a little too close.

KAISER: Move back, please, Tirpitz. You are in my line of vision.

TIRPITZ: *(Moving behind the monarch.)* Apologies, your Majesty! Do excuse me! But as I was saying, Moltke and I tried really hard to avoid discussing politics with the British.

KAISER: I doubt you could have, anyway. There was no one with that kind of authority.

TIRPITZ has the pleasant smile and the stupidity of one who thinks himself very funny and winning. He wants to answer, but before he can utter a word the KAISER rants:

KAISER: Three times I asked them to send Churchill. I mean, he's been my guest on two at the Autumn manoeuvres. So why not now when he's Lord of the Admiralty?... I'll tell you why, gentlemen. He's too embarrassed to show his face when he's holding the knife to stab us with. What other reason is there? And that nonsense last year...that we and the British suspend shipbuilding for an entire year! Whoever heard of anything more stupid or insulting?... And now my spies inform me that, instead of Autumn manoeuvres, he wants a trial mobilisation.

The KAISER becomes so excited that he gets up quickly. He repeats the phrase he finds so appalling.

Have you ever heard the like? A trial mobilisation! Imagine if I ordered that. 'No autumn manoeuvres this year, good people! We'll have a trial mobilisation instead!' I'd be assassinated.

He sits down, takes up his paintbrush again and continues to paint.

TIRPITZ: All the same your Majesty, you did agree to meet him once in Kiel…

KAISER: *(Angrily.)* More than 'agree', Tirpitz. I wanted him to come.

TIRPITZ: I have to say, I'd have found it difficult. The man is such an adventurer.

KAISER: What exactly do you mean, an 'adventurer'?

TIRPITZ: Well, didn't he travel the world as a young man? Whenever he got a whiff of war, there he was…as a journalist, admittedly.

KAISER: And he wrote some interesting books! Are you able to say, Moltke, that the people you command have had as much experience of modern warfare? Churchill was in the thick of it in the Boer War.

MOLTKE: I'm afraid we do not, your Majesty. But if I may say so, I'd sleep much easier if you too conducted a trial mobilisation. It would tell us if we are ready to march.

KAISER: *(Still very absorbed in his painting.)* What's that, Julius? Sleep easier? You remind me of Philip Eulenburg. He slept quite well, I'm told…with ten members of my staff!

TIRPITZ and MOLTKE laugh at the KAISER's little joke.

MOLTKE turns and gestures to the background, which is hardly visible because PROFESSOR WILLY STÖWER, the painter of maritime scenes, has a large canvas on his easel and is painting the black-looking silhouettes of the English visitors' ships, which are anchored in Kiel harbour.

MOLTKE: Well at least the British are here at Kiel Week. The first time in 19 years. It must be a positive sign.

KAISER: *(Shrugs.)* Perhaps, if Churchill were here too. But he's not. And neither is Briand!

TIRPITZ: *(Glancing at MOLTKE, as if to suggest that the KAISER is insane.)* If I may say so your Majesty, what use would a past French Premier be to us?

KAISER: *(Amazed at the stupidity of TIRPITZ's question.)* You can't be serious, Tirpitz! The present Premier would never come. Have you read the newspapers lately? He and the President are soon to visit the Tsar. No one visits us anymore! *(Furious, he puts his paintbrush down again.)* And that, gentlemen, could and should have been avoided. Our Foreign Office is incompetent, entirely to blame for this! What must the British have thought when Haldane came here to discuss the speed of ship-building, and our Foreign Secretary did a disappearing act – off on a jaunt with his girlfriend. I tell you this: if he hadn't put an end to himself, I'd have done it for him! Our Chancellor thought he was brave, simply because he was so cold – as cold as ten dogs' noses!

MOLTKE: I've often wondered how Churchill justified not building ships – I mean to the owners and the workers.

TIRPITZ: *(Interjects.)* Especially the people producing steel!

MOLTKE: Not a single ship for a whole year!

TIRPITZ: While your Majesty's fleet kept men in full employment in the Ruhr and Upper Silesia – more, in fact, than in coalmining.

KAISER: *(Absorbed in his painting, grumbling.)* Yes, yes, Tirpitz, I know. But you, Julius, are being naïve. You think Churchill's going to tell us how he keeps his workers happy? Of course he won't! But he'll manage it in different ways. He'll have them building smaller vessels. He'll arm his merchant ships – my spies confirm it. He'll increase the fire power of older ships, change from coal to oil. So not to worry, Julius. He'll keep the owners happy, the money rolling in.

TIRPITZ: May I make a suggestion, your Majesty. Why not send out a press release? 'Churchill secretly arming merchant and passenger shipping'.

KAISER: Absolutely not! We do that and our men over there
– our only man over there – be exposed… Stöwer! Come
over here! I want you to tell me the truth. Is this that much
worse than yours?

STÖWER: *(In a military voice.)* Coming, your Majesty! Just a
moment!

TIRPITZ: *(Quickly, before STÖWER, who is still wiping his hands,
comes across.)* If I may say so, your Majesty, your treatment
of air and light is quite ingenious, much more true to
marine colours than oil painting, including Professor
Stöwer's. Watercolour, as your Majesty proves, is much
more marine specific than oils…though I am not an expert.

*STÖWER is a small, intense man with a Kaiser-like moustache, its
ends pointing towards his eyes. It was TIRPITZ who first brought
him on board. This is his fifteenth trip with the KAISER.*

STÖWER: Couldn't agree more, Admiral. Not amateurish
at all! On the contrary, quite expert. He is completely
correct, your Majesty. It is such a joy to see how you paint.
Aquarelle is such a delicate and difficult medium.

KAISER: *(Smiling benignly.)* Perhaps so, Professor. But if you
were not on board, I could never achieve all this. Your work
inspires me. Perhaps I should sign my painting 'Stöwer'.

*STÖWER is understandably shocked at the thought the KAISER would
honour him by signing his name in this way.*

STÖWER: *(Hastily.)* Oh, please, your Majesty! Your 'Sea Battle'
is your own intellectual property!

KAISER: *(Laughs happily.)* Come, now, Professor. You flatter
me. You know very well I saw your painting of the
Tsushima Sea Battle at your studio.

STÖWER: Indeed you did! But that does not devalue your
work. What I see before me is a new Tsushima, a quite
original painting. May I remind your Majesty that I too
base work on photographs. As for yourself, how else could
you paint this subject? None of us were present when the
Japanese engaged the Russian ships.

KAISER: Quite true, Professor. But tell me, why are you painting British ships, immortalizing in oils? Don't you realize I find it rather provocative?

STÖWER: *(Taken aback.)* Believe me, your Majesty, that is not my intention. On the contrary, I am attempting to paint a naval battle in which we defeat the British. I share the dream of every loyal German. How could I ever 'immortalize' the fleet of the treacherous British in the presence of your Majesty? I feel my painting might even dissuade the British from sailing into Swinemünde Bay ever again. I witnessed it, you know, in 1904.

KAISER: Yes, yes, Stöwer, I understand. Now tell me. Is my painting complete? Or should I add some grey to the sky?

STÖWER: *(Quickly.)* Not at all, your Majesty. The painting is perfect. My advice is therefore not a stroke more.

KAISER: *(Sceptical.)* Are you quite sure? You see this ship here, burning from stern to bridge? Could a child be certain it's a Russian ship, not a Japanese?

STÖWER: Of course, your Majesty. The painting is extremely accurate. The details of the Russian ship are very clear.

KAISER: That chap down there! What does he want? There aren't dispatches on a Sunday!

The KAISER calls out to WEIZSÄCKER, who has run to collect the message:

No mail today! It's Kiel Week, for God's sake! Has the fellow got St. Vitus' dance? What the hell's going on?

WEIZSÄCKER, who is commanding officer of the deck, attempts to catch a silver cigarette case thrown up to him from the dispatch boat by DEATH, but it falls on deck and he has to bend down in order to retrieve it. He opens it and passes the message it contains to the KAISER.

WEIZSÄCKER: I'm sorry, your Majesty. It seems it's urgent.

KAISER: Very well. Give it here.

He rips open the telegram. Seldom is he lost for words, but on this occasion he is speechless. TIRPITZ and MOLTKE realise that this is no ordinary telegram.

The KAISER hands it to MOLTKE. He reads the one sentence and hands it to TIRPITZ.

MOLTKE: Sarajevo. Franz Ferdinand and his wife murdered! He was our loyal ally! What do we do now?

The KAISER indicates that WEIZSÄCKER should wait. Seeing that the KAISER wishes to write a message, WEIZSÄCKER takes a notepad from his pocket and salutes. The KAISER dictates.

KAISER: The telegram's to go via the chancellery, you understand? Take this down! 'To his Imperial Majesty, Vienna... My dear Franz Joseph. Myself, the Empress and my entire people feel the deepest shock at the news of this wicked murder. We share your family's grief, as well as the grief of the Austro-Hungarian people...' No, wait! Don't send it yet! Come back in half an hour. In the meantime, inform the Empress and call off Kiel Week... Inform our English visitors too. Suggest they go home!

WEIZSÄCKER: Yes, your Majesty. Inform Her Majesty the Empress, call off Kiel Week, suggest British return home. At once, sir.

Then WEIZSÄCKER clicks his heels, salutes and bows.

KAISER: *(As WEIZSÄCKER exits.)* All flags are to fly at half-mast, in Kiel too – no, I correct myself...in the entire Reich... Thank you! No doubt his father will want him in the Imperial Crypt. Not the fat wife, though! Can't see him doing that! Such a smart, scheming woman! My wife I must have been the only ones who treated her as an equal, as an Archduchess. That's why Franz Ferdinand liked us. His father didn't approve, of course. I remember his mother telling him in the father's presence: 'Marry the woman you love, my boy. If you do not, your children will be ugly'. Heaven forbid, they'll be orphans now! I doubt that many will share their grief. And little Karl will soon be Emperor. A fate worse than death! He'd be better off as a village postman! All this on such a lovely day! I feel so cold! As the British say: 'Fortune may have pretty curls, but the back of her head is bald'.

TIRPITZ: The telegram says the assassins have been arrested. Serbians, it seems. You think it's true or mere hearsay?

KAISER: Those who aim the gun are seldom the only ones responsible. But I'm sure Vienna will seek justice for this atrocity. And we shall side with them. How can we not? If my eldest son were shot by French nationalists, I'd do the same.

STÖWER has moved upstage and is packing up his easel. Where he was painting there is now a sailor played by DEATH, his back to the KAISER and the stalls. He is signalling with flags, communicating the news of the Archduke's death and the KAISER's order to cancel Kiel Week.

Look at you both, dressed up to the nines! You should change. No need to pander to our guests anymore.

MOLTKE: May I suggest, your Highness, that we stay in uniform. You said yourself that Vienna will take action against Belgrade.

TIRPITZ: And that will mean a wider war. Russia will not stand by if Serbia is attacked.

KAISER: Gentlemen, you think the Tsar will side with those who've murdered a future king?

TIRPITZ: But you've always said the Tsar is rather like a cork, at the mercy of the waves. He may not be the one who makes the decisions.

KAISER: Quite possibly. But Franz Joseph was not so fond of his son that he will want to march on Belgrade.

MOLTKE: Permission to speak, your Majesty. I suggest we should not try to dissuade Vienna from taking action. We should encourage her. If she does not respond to this, she will become a laughing stock. Brutal sanctions could be imposed, of course, but war would be a better option – much better now than in two years' time. The position is this: we have superior artillery. France and Russia are short of howitzers. We have superior rifles, though in two years' time the French will have them too. At present the French cavalry is badly trained, ours is not. The weather favours us, the crops are harvested, and the new recruits have completed their training. Success would be ours.

KAISER: *(Looks at him sheepishly. He feels he should reject MOLTKE's advice, but he knows he is really too weak to do so. And, like all weak men, he fears being regarded as one.)* Very convincing, Moltke, but tell me this. A Frenchman said recently that 40 million French soldiers would be stronger than 70 million Germans.

TIRPITZ: And the fleet, your Majesty. It could stop the British crossing into France – should they become involved, that is.

KAISER: And how many British will try to fight in France?

MOLTKE: According to the latest figures, 160,000, possibly fewer. But in my opinion, the fleet should not be involved. The British should be allowed to enter France. They will then be trapped there. We could finish all of them off.

TIRPITZ: If the fleet is not to be involved, how can it justify its existence?

KAISER: *(Waves this away.)* It does enough already. It protects our coastline. It prevents the British sending supplies to the Russians via the Baltic Sea! Even so, you two gentlemen seem to think that war is inevitable.

TIRPITZ: Not inevitable, your Majesty. Simply desirable.

MOLTKE: And because our numbers are inferior, surprise is the best form of attack.

TIRPITZ: Pre-emptive warfare, Majesty. If we do nothing, Austria will cease to be an ally. If we do something, it will test the entente. And if they move against us, it will prove that that was always their intention. I agree with my colleague: better now than in two years' time!

KAISER: Gentlemen, I have to remind you of the words of someone the journalists constantly refer to. I mean, of course, the all-knowing, infallible Bismarck. Note what he said: 'Even if we succeed now, the war will always be ahead of us, never behind us'. And so it is today. Russia and France will always be a threat. We cannot alter geography.

The KAISER is already smoking his second cigarette. MOLTKE has taken the golden case that the KAISER has produced from his pocket, given him a cigarette and then a light.

TIRPITZ: As you well know, your Majesty, Bismarck neglected to take from France the iron-producing region of Longwy-Briey. But if you succeed in doing so, together with three ports on the Atlantic coast...

KAISER: *(Sarcastic.)* Only three, Tirpitz!

TIRPITZ: The French will still be our neighbours, but neighbours with only one good hand, considerably weakened.

A terrible slip of the tongue: the phrase seems to have slipped unintentionally out of TIRPITZ's mouth as a result of seeing the KAISER's withered left arm, which obliged MOLTKE to give him the cigarette. The KAISER looks at TIRPITZ seriously, but manages to smile and even make a joke.

KAISER: You fail to see, Tirpitz, that, as in my case, a one-armed man can still shoot.

TIRPITZ: *(Skating over the comment, though he is greatly embarrassed.)* Of course, but how well will the French shoot if they are defeated and forced to buy all their steel from us?

MOLTKE: I must say I agree with the Admiral about the Western Front. As for Russia, I believe Bismarck was right. We should take nothing from them. Did not Frederick the Great state in his will that we should never march on Russia?

KAISER: Indeed he did. He considered Karl of Sweden an utter fool for invading the Ukraine.

MOLTKE: A German victory, your Majesty, would guarantee lasting peace, not least when you have annexed Luxembourg and part of Belgium.

KAISER: Perhaps so, Moltke. But one should never share out the bear-skin before the hunt. Assuming, of course, that the hunt takes place.

MOLTKE: The hunt is inevitable, your Majesty. Sarajevo was a gift from God!

KAISER: It may be a gift, Moltke. From God, I'm not so sure. Anyway, I need a piss.

INTERMISSION

DEATH returns. Looks at the audience. The sound of the machine begins – first intermittently, then increasing, until by the end, it's nearly drowning him out.

DEATH: The Machine is gearing up
I can feel this flesh a-tremble
Each pact is signed
The lines are drawn
The dogs are baying
Hear them cry?
See the ravens
Faster circle
Rats come running
Poised to feed
Here it comes
Here comes the cutter
It's coming for you
Listen, listen, hear it call
Here comes the cutter
Coming for you
Listen listen hear it call –
Blood
Blood
Blood

The cries of 'Blood' are eclipsed by the sounds of bullets, machine guns, tanks getting nearer – there is a climax of sound, then a sudden blackout.

INTERVAL

Act Two

A CHORALE OF BALANCES

DEATH: *(As a skeleton, sings and trumpets.)*
They idolise their heroes,
The famous they adore,
But they don't know the names of the millions,
Who were thrown on the fire like coal.

They don't know the soldiers who fell
Who drew their last desperate breath,
On the orders of heartless butchers,
Condemned to inglorious death.

Millions put through the grinder,
In school taught to be patriots,
Encouraged in church by the preachers,
Not knowing that they would be lost.

The family weeps for the victims.
They did their bit for their king,
But they were just sheep to the slaughter,
Discarded like cheap little things.

The ones who deserve to die
Are those who sent them to fight,
Who profited from all the chaos,
And claimed they were in the right.

They stayed away from the fighting –
They considered that nine million dead
Would vastly improve their finances.
The death toll means nothing to them.

A soldier to them's just a number,
They'd rather not think what they've done;
While friend and foe lie dead together,
Their beat plays on a hollowed-out drum.
He indicates his heart.

A soldier to them's just a number,
They'd rather not think what they've done;
While friend and foe lie dead together,
Their hearts are hollowed out drums.

SCENE 7
BELGRADE: THE ULTIMATUM
Austrian Embassy in Belgrade
10 July 1914

A magnificently panelled room in the Austrian Embassy in Belgrade. GIESL VON GIESLINGEN is hastily packing up his documents into his bags. He is dressed casually in light grey, his clothes made from the finest English cloth. He wears a large black ribbon on his right arm, and his wide tie is also black.

DEATH: The Imperial Austrian Embassy in Belgrade. Ambassador Vladimir Baron Giesel von Gieslingen knows the Russians are coming for him. They've forewarned him by telephone.

The Russian Ambassador BARON NICHOLAS GENRIKHOVICH HARTWIG enters.

His Excellency the Ambassador for His Imperial Majesty the Tsar of Russia!

DEATH exits, closing the massive doors behind him.

GIESL: Ambassador! This is a surprise! I wasn't expecting you for another week or two.

HARTWIG: *(Taking GIESL's outstretched hand.)* My dear General, the murder of the Archduke and his wife came as a complete shock. The Tsar offers his condolences, as indeed do I. However, my dear Giesl – and please understand that I say this as a friend, not as the Tsar's ambassador – your ultimatum to Serbia has undoubtedly darkened the horizon. Six years ago you seized Bosnia and Herzegovina from Russian protection. This seems at least as serious.

GIESL offers HARTWIG a cigarette from a silver cigarette case, who declines but is unable to speak because a powerful cough is almost tearing him apart.

GIESL: My dear best Hartwig, am I to think that the Tsar weeps because the crown prince has been murdered, or that he laughs because it happened in Serbia? Does he really wish to protect murderers?

HARTWIG: When the news arrived from Sarajevo 12 days ago, I literally screamed: 'God grant us the murderer is not a Serbian!'

GIESL: So they tell me, Excellency. But I'm told too that the embassy was brightly lit until the early hours, as if it were the Tsar's birthday, not the occasion of a murder!

HARTWIG: You are mistaken, my friend. Guests had already arrived from abroad. What was I supposed to do? Send them away because I'd lost my appetite? As for being 'brightly lit', of course we had the lights on. Was I to entertain my guests in the dark? I think Vienna should understand one thing, Giesl – Serbians will always fight to unite Bosnia and Herzegovina with Belgrade. These two provinces you stole – I repeat, stole – belong to Serbia.

GIESL: *(Standing, more agitated, walking back and forth. He knows that HARTWIG is right.)* So you think that the best way to unify Bosnia with Belgrade is shooting our crown prince?

HARTWIG is friendly but determined. He could well have been at least a co-conspirator in the assassination.

HARTWIG: Are we talking of politics, Giesl, or simply murder? One is never a means to the other… Would Vienna think of taking military measures simply to avenge a murder? It's a matter for the local police. You shouldn't think that the Serbian government…

GIESL: I'm sorry, Hartwig. If the government did not supply the murderers with cyanide, who did? A criminal can buy a revolver on the street, but cyanide? And who supported these young men in Sarajevo for weeks on end?

HARTWIG: No doubt there were backers, but not the government, I assure you.

GIESL: Nevertheless, the Serbian government wishes to recover those two provinces. It is their stated aim. So how can they achieve it without going to war?

HARTWIG: An assassination does not lead to war, Giesl! To start a war because the crown prince was murdered is sheer madness.

GIESL: So what should Austria do in the opinion of the
Russian ambassador? Apologize for its existence?

HARTWIG: Ensure the streets are more secure when a new
crown prince visits Sarajevo… You need to understand,
Giesl, that Bosnia and Herzegovina are a poisoned chalice.
These two teeth in Austria's mouth are infecting the rest.
Believe me, Giesl, this is the truth.

*HARTWIG says this with such apparent sincerity that he probably
believes it himself at that moment.*

GIESL: *(Sadly.)* I know you mean well, Hartwig, but you
exaggerate Austria's opposition to Serbia. Are you aware
that it was my predecessor who managed to obtain from
the King of Milan a pardon for the Serbian traitor – I mean
Pašić, of course, who is not only Premier today, but also
the richest man in Serbia?

HARTWIG: *(Another fit of coughing that almost splits him in two.)*
don't understand, my friend. What has a politician's wealth
to do with the matter in hand?

GIESL: A great deal, sir. His fortune comes from sweeteners
paid to him by French arms manufacturers…to ensure
Serbia purchases every piece of junk they produce. The
French themselves have no use for it, even in their North
African police stations.

HARTWIG: *(Laughing loudly.)* Come, come, Giesl! The Serbs
had great success with their French weapons. If Pašić
armed his people so well, he deserves to prosper.

GIESL: And how much did they pay him, so that, as head of
the Black Hand…

HARTWIG: Can you prove that he is?

GIESL: In every country the Head of State is always Head of
the Secret Service. I wouldn't be surprised if he arranged
for those murderers to go to Sarajevo. Serbia wants war
because it wants its provinces back. And the only way to
achieve that is to see Austria cease to be a major power.

HARTWIG puts his hand on his heart.

GIESL: Are you all right, Excellency?

HARTWIG: *(Taking out a handkerchief and going to the window.)* Yes, yes. I'm quite all right. It's just that it's so hot in here. If I could have some mineral water…

GIESL: *(Ringing the bell.)* Champagne, if you prefer.

DEATH (as the SERVANT) is already at the door.

HARTWIG: No, no, just mineral water, please.

GIESL: *(Sharply.)* Mineral water, then. Make sure it's cold!

DEATH exits. HARTWIG leans on the windowsill. He gasps for breath, his words come slowly.

HARTWIG: My friend…you say the Serbian Premier…is in the pocket of Parisian weapons manufacturers… I say so what? We both know that wars aren't caused…by arms manufacturers wanting to increase their dividends.

GIESL: I'm not so sure. A capitalist society might well claim it can survive without wars, but it hasn't been proved to date.

HARTWIG: I am no economist… You must, however, admit… that diplomats are not ruled by industry… And they are the people who decide…whether or not there will be war.

DEATH enters with glasses and an ice-bucket containing a bottle of mineral water. He fills the glass.

HARTWIG guzzles it and immediately holds his glass out for more. The conversation continues uninterrupted.

HARTWIG: In any case, Giesl, Pašić can buy as many cannons as he wishes from the French, but the decision to use them still comes from St. Petersburg. And I can promise you, as an officer of the Tsar, that Russia will not march if Austria does not attack Serbia. My word of honour!

GIESL: But 'attack' is a rather ambiguous word. So what should we do? Thank the Serbs for removing our heir to the throne. Even if his wife was something of a liability.

HARTWIG: You seem not to want to understand… If Austria invades Serbia, Russia will invade Austria. Germany will, of course, support Austria and France Russia. As for the British, they may become involved too. But peace…let's have peace…

First the bottle and the glass fall, for HARTWIG has taken the bottle out of the ice-bucket in order to serve himself. Broken glass flies everywhere. HARTWIG crumples to his knees and falls. Still jerking, he lies on the wooden floor, dies.

GIESL: *(Calls out without moving.)* Hartwig! God! Hartwig!

GIESL goes to him, turns him over, cannot bear to look into those wide-open eyes. He steps back from the body, rushes to the door.

GIESL: A doctor! Call a doctor!

He comes back to the body. DEATH follows him and tries to lift HARTWIG. GIESL makes no effort to help. He hisses at DEATH.

GIESL: For God's sake, a doctor! Now!

DEATH: I'll get him into the car. Help me!

GIESL: What the hell are you doing? Leave him!

The slightly built DEATH stops trying to lift the dead body. But GIESL stares at it expressionless. DEATH kneels again to open the collar of frock-coat.

GIESL: The telephone, man! No, find my secretary. He can do it. You call the Russians! Tell them we have bad news…just that….bad news.

DEATH: *(Exiting.)* At once, your Excellency.

GIESL is already reaching for his broad-rimmed hat and stick. DEATH, who in response to each order just silently nodded his head, goes out quickly.

GIESL, hat and stick in hand, ready to leave, steps up to the corpse one more time.

GIESL: The first Russian to fall in the war he always wanted… I think his last word was 'peace'. He said 'peace', but he meant 'war'. I didn't know you could die of a lie.

MONOLOGUE OF A SOPHISTICATED MUNITIONS MANUFACTURER

DEATH as a sophisticated weapons manufacturer – nationality is unimportant – approaches the audience, doffs his top hat and secures his monocle.

DEATH: The Industry could not have been
   In better hands throughout the war
   Lots of money to be made
   Big dividends that's for sure

   The ladies make our splendid arms
   And while they pump out those grenades

The little girls have work assured.
Dollars girls to arm brigades

With mouths to feed they need the work
Big daddy here will see them right
But when the church bells start to peal
They'll be back at home and out of sight.

The weekly wage I pay the girls,
Is the same as retired generals skim
From makers of their arms like me,
Commission given from us given to them

For their services can you believe.
I know – it's amazing what war can do
They are the criminals it sure ain't me
It's them if anyone who should be sued

(Spoken, after the music ends.) Why are you looking at me like that?

What did I do?

SCENE 8
AMERICAN DOLLARS FOR BLOOD
The new wing of the Washington National Gallery
4 May 1915

A medium-sized room in the Washington National Gallery. Enter the industrial merchant HENRY STIMSON. His high top hat is as much part of his everyday attire as the suit, the white spats and the Spanish cane with ivory handle. He also has a large pearl in his wide blue tie under his stiff collar as well as a long watch chain over his waistcoat. This intelligent man is immortalising himself by building up a gallery.

Enter a DIRECTOR of the gallery. He too is wearing a suit, because he has been given advance notice of this patron's visit.

DIRECTOR: So here it is, Mr Stimson. I've had it cleared, though I don't assume you'll be giving us paintings to fill the space entirely…

STIMSON: Impressive! There must be room for a dozen paintings…God, where is my daughter? *(Upset, he looks at his pocket watch.)* I should tell you, sir, if I can get my hands on a couple of dozen, I'll be building my own private gallery…

like my friend, Henry Frick. It's a difficult thing buying pictures. Much easier buying a hat, even a corporation. Not everyone's willing to part with a Leonardo…

DIRECTOR: *(Smiling.)* I'm sure they aren't. I'm amazed that you've managed to buy so many. And you might still get another Renoir, seeing he's still alive… You see here, Mr Stimson. It's got your nameplate.

One of the four paintings is now unwrapped. At the bottom of the frame there is a small silver plate, the business card of the donor. The DIRECTOR steps back to admire the painting.

STIMSON: Ah, yes. But do remember. It's in no way legally binding. My lawyers will be here at 11 o'clock, just to make sure you know the pictures are a loan, nothing more. The paintings can remain here, in Washington, just so my kids won't be fighting over them. You see, sir, you can share out a business quite easily, but paintings are a different kettle of fish. You leave your daughter a Goya, your son a Leonardo. Nothing but trouble!

DIRECTOR: *(Joining in his laughter.)* Indeed! I quite understand, Mr Stimson. And we, of course, are extremely grateful. Speaking of which, I wonder if you'd be willing to give a little talk about the paintings.

STIMSON takes off his top hat, puts his cane to one side, and sits in an armchair as the third painting is revealed.

STIMSON: I'm afraid not, sir. I'm no expert. You see, I rely entirely on a handful of wealthy and influential Europeans. In any case, your admiration is somewhat misplaced. If I don't donate the pictures, they'd all be in the auction house before I'm in the ground. You know how ungrateful children can be. When they've ruined my business, the paintings will still be here. I'll be thought of as public spirited, don't you think?

What STIMSON has donated to the gallery is quite breath-taking: a variation on Manet's 'Blue Venice', Renoir's sketch of Tilla Durieux, Goya's painting of a man with a rearing horse, and Leonardo's large study of five apostle heads from his most famous fresco, 'The Last Supper'.

The ATTENDANTS have unpacked the paintings and want to hang them, but are unsure of the order in which to do so. Another ATTENDANT enters.

ATTENDANT: Excuse me, sir. Three men want to see you in your office.

STIMSON: That'll be the lawyers, 11 o'clock on the dot. *(To the DIRECTOR.)* If you don't mind, sir, I'll wait here for my daughter…

DIRECTOR: Of course! I'll get the loan certificate prepared. Please arrange the pictures as you see fit.

The DIRECTOR exits.

STIMSON: The Leonardo in the middle, maybe – though you can't say the middle when there are four… No, no! We'll have the Leonardo on its own…some distance from the others. Yes, try it there!

He gestures to the men lifting the heavy picture. As STIMSON steps back, his daughter MARGOT STIMSON drifts in. Dressed not so much elegantly, but more like a middle-class woman taking tram to work, she tenderly touches the back of her father's neck and reveals her annoyance with the ATTENDANT chasing her.

MARGOT: You believe me now? I told you he's my father!

STIMSON: *(Turns around, delighted.)* Margot! I've been waiting half an hour!

The ATTENDANT retreats.

MARGOT: *(Amused.)* That's my dad! Always complaining how long you have to wait!

STIMSON: *(Good humoured.)* Haste may not be a virtue, my dear, but neither is lateness. If you go to war, you have to be on time! Help me arrange these pictures. What do you think? Manet to the left next to Renoir, or…

MARGOT: The two impressionists on either end, Goya to the right next to Leonardo.

STIMSON: *(To the ATTENDANTS.)* You heard the lady. Where women have their say, how can men not obey? *(To MARGOT.)* Aren't you sorry I'm donating the paintings?

MARGOT: *(Shrugging.)* Why would I be? Thousands can enjoy them here. Sorry I kept you waiting. I wanted to pick up my ticket at the Cunard-Line, so I could change my cabin if I didn't like it.

STIMSON: Show me the ticket.

MARGOT produces the ticket from her pocket book with mild bewilderment, gives it to him.

MARGOT: Come with me if you want. Had to take a suite. There'd be plenty of room.

STIMSON glances at the workers, but they are busy. He pushes his daughter into the armchair, close to the front of the stage. He talks quietly, putting the ticket in his coat pocket.

STIMSON: You can't go on that ship. She's going to be sunk. Not this time maybe, but sunk for sure. She's British bait, Margot, loaded with ammunition. You need to take some harmless Norwegian or Spanish vessel.

MARGOT resists his argument, puts her hand in her father's pocket, fights with him over the ticket.

MARGOT: *(Loudly.)* Dad, stop being paranoid!

STIMSON, by far the stronger, amusedly takes the ticket from his outer pocket, where his daughter can get hold of it, and puts it in his inner pocket.

STIMSON: *(Quietly.)* Listen to me! I've been told officially that under no circumstances should I sail on the Lusitania.

Now loudly, much more jovial for the benefit of the ATTENDANTS. He gives each of them a large tip. They doff their caps, mumbling their thanks. STIMSON waves them away, wanting to be alone with his daughter.

STIMSON: Is this OK, the way we've arranged them? Bye! Thank you!

He closes the door behind the exiting ATTENDANTS.

STIMSON: Listen to me for once!

MARGOT: Dad, I am going to Europe. I am going to join Miss Cavell to work in her field hospital. You can't stop me! But I'll go to the harbour. I'll hand out leaflets telling the passengers why they shouldn't be on the Lusitania.

STIMSON: You can't do that! You really can't!

MARGOT: Why not? It's a simple choice. Disappoint my father or tell the passengers that the ship will be sunk... I imagine to make sure our country enters the war.

STIMSON: If the Germans take the bait, it shows how stupid they are. But they will! They'll sink the world's biggest passenger liner even though they know there are women and children on board – all of them citizens of a country they are still at peace with.

MARGOT: That makes it more important that I'm there tomorrow. I'll tell them everything I know.

STIMSON: Can't you see how naïve this is? You'll be arrested. They don't wear kid gloves, you know. You want to go to France to work as a nurse. OK, I admire that. You're a stubborn person, like me.

He smiles wearily, resigned to the situation, afraid that the girl he loves will be killed.

MARGOT: Can't you see, Dad? Can't you see that you've made us so ashamed that we can't even face people, can't even look people in the eye? Just look at you! All the paintings do is ease your conscience!

STIMSON: Well at least you admit I have a conscience.

MARGOT: I suppose it makes you feel you are doing something for the common good. But it's only 20% of what you make from the war.

STIMSON: Your figures aren't so good, Margot. You used to be better when you worked for me.

MARGOT: It took me a while to find out what you were really like.

STIMSON: I don't understand these accusations.

MARGOT: Well, you're one of the biggest arms dealers in recorded history.

STIMSON: You have such a nice way of putting things!

MARGOT: Why? Am I wrong?

STIMSON: You know, I was five years younger than you are now when my father died. And what did he leave me? A worn-out pair of pants and the need to feed my mother and my two sisters. Nowadays I feed 107,000 families! And

I tell you this – some of Henry Ford's ideas may have been crazy, but he got one thing right: look after your workers and they won't let you down! So I keep them happy.

MARGOT: How can you compare yourself with Uncle Henry? He makes everyone's dreams come true. They want to drive cars even more than they want sex! But your people…a woman on your assembly line…she'll be dead before she's forty, killed by the metal and the chemicals she has to work with. What's she supposed to feed her family with? Shells from your factory?

One senses that STIMSON wants to stop this conversation, but not because his daughter is right. He is not that easily beaten, and he is not going to be affected by just one argument:

STIMSON: My women make other things, as you well know. Tins for canned meat, or for the soup they serve at the Ritz? That's how lucky they are! They earn a decent living!

MARGOT: Maybe they do, but tin cans don't finance your arms industry. You only make them to cover up, so people can't say what kind of industrialist you really are… As for the paintings and the hospitals you give money to, do they make up for the millions who, thanks to you, will die on the battlefields of Europe? I worked for you once, so I know what you do!

STIMSON: Margot, you're a clever woman. You could take over from me. But there's something I have to tell you I've not told anyone else… The thing is…it seems likely, well, maybe more than likely…that…I've got cancer…which means I haven't got long. That's what they tell me… But I've kept it from your mother. You aren't to tell her.

MARGOT: What? Who told you this? For heaven's sake, Dad! You look perfectly well.

STIMSON: I'd really rather not talk about it. Maybe it's a wrong diagnosis. They make mistakes, you know.

MARGOT: *(Kisses him.)* You have to see Goldberg. He can do a biopsy. God! I don't believe this!

STIMSON: *(Kissing her.)* Anyway, let's not talk about it. There's something else I want to say. After the war, we wouldn't be making ammunition any more. You could be like your Uncle du Pont. He's planning to build an automobile factory, calling it General Motors. It's going to employ thousands. You could do something similar, get people into work. Don't you see? It's so much better than being a nurse.

MARGOT: *(Resolutely.)* Father, you can be very persuasive, but this cancer thing…

STIMSON: Don't you believe me?

MARGOT: Maybe I do, maybe I don't. You know, I love you in spite of all this. I worked for you for a long time, despite my principles.

STIMSON: You've got a good nose for business, Margot.

MARGOT: But everything's different now. The shells you make… it means America's backing the biggest slaughter we've ever seen. Millions of innocent Europeans dead…and partly because of you! As for this plan to get people employed, you think I believe that? All you do now is pay someone off so he can eat and stab someone else in the back. It's bullshit!

STIMSON: *(In a voice which reveals his embarrassment.)* So you think I'm to blame for the war in Europe! Well, dammit, I'm not, and neither is America. If we stop making weapons, you think one bullet less will be fired? Of course not! The war won't be a day shorter. So why don't you do what I say and stop being so damned self-righteous? We need to help defeat those crazy Germans!

MARGOT: But they've done nothing to us! Nothing!

STIMSON: Not yet. But believe me, they will!

MARGOT: The Germans aren't necessarily the aggressors. That letter the President showed you. He knew from Colonel House that England was ready to invade Germany. And Russia and France would be ready too. Sarajevo wasn't the cause of the war. It gave the others the opportunity.

STIMSON: *(Solicitous, proud of the clever daughter he adores, the only person who is close to him.)* Margot, if you stay with me, I promise you one thing. You'll have nothing to do with munitions.

MARGOT: Too late, Father. I'm leaving. Some of us prefer to expose ourselves to war, not draw up plans so others can be butchered. Anyway, I hope you don't really have cancer. For Mother's sake!

She kisses him, and he holds her tight.

A knock at the door.

STIMSON: Yes, what is it?

He goes to the door, opens it. Outside is a gallery ATTENDANT. He hands over a telegram.

ATTENDANT: A telegram for your daughter, Mr Stimson.

MARGOT: *(Surprised.)* For me? Thank you!

She hands the telegram to her father.

MARGOT: It's from the German embassy. I can't think why.

STIMSON: *(To the ATTENDANT.)* Could you call the Director, please.

MARGOT has opened her pocket book, takes out a dollar bill and gives it to the ATTENDANT, who mumbles his thanks, bows and exits.

MARGOT: Thank you… See what it says.

STIMSON hands the telegram back to her.

STIMSON: I know what it says. The ambassador's written to everyone booked on the Lusitania. He's telling them not to go on board. Some haven't listened, of course.

She nods and, having read the telegram, hands it once more to her father.

MARGOT: I've told you. I'll go on another ship. You could come with me, see for yourself what your shells are doing. It might even change your mind.

STIMSON is not unimpressed, but the DIRECTOR has just entered and come to his aid.

DIRECTOR: You want to see me, Mr Stimson.

STIMSON: Thank you. I've arranged the paintings…with my daughter's help. I'd like your opinion.

DIRECTOR: *(Bowing.)* Excellent, Mr Stimson. I'll take a look.

ONE GONE DOWN WITH THE LUSITANIA

A woman around thirty years old, soaking wet, her hair bedraggled. She wears a large life-belt, which displays the name HMS Lusitania. Her simple clothes are those of a maid.

VICTIM: We weren't in the least worried when the Lusitania started to speed up off the coast of Ireland. Our ship wasn't carrying troops, the Germans knew from the passenger list we were all civilians. Because we was all civvies, we'd been alright about the munitions coming on board in New York. New York was neutral. We didn't think for a minute it was a problem. Even though it slowed the ship down. They was bound for Britain. For our war effort. And we weren't soldiers so, so what? We thought that made us safe. So when we got to Ireland and she started to speed up, we didn't think for a minute it was a problem. We didn't think for a minute she was trying to escape German submarines.

We didn't know someone in our government wanted to provoke the Germans. A hundred and fifty American citizens went down when we sunk. A hundred and fifty dead citizens would be enough to bring the USA into the war. Who would have thought they would swallow that bait.

We knew the Hun were evil enough to drop bombs from airships onto women and children. But no one thought they would stoop this low. The world was horrified by their cowardice. Though that's no consolation to us dead. The torpedo that got us killed, killed almost as many as the iceberg that sunk the Titanic.

After it hit, the ship sank like a stone. The exploding ammunition put half the lifeboats out of action. At the time I was on the upper deck with my mistress, at least I wasn't down below.

I managed to get into the water and swim far enough out to avoid being pulled down by the undertow. There were hundreds of people trying to keep afloat, clinging to pieces of debris. We saw things which showed us human nature at its worst.

A rescue boat, the Juno, came towards us. I can't describe the joy I felt, but then it turned and sped away. Someone gave the order to let us drown.

It must have been hours later I saw another boat. But I'd drifted too far away to be seen. And I was too tired to even wave. I don't know how long I'd been in the water…eight, nine, ten hours. Thing is, you die very slowly out there.

I tried to defend my eyes from the seagulls. They swoop down, you see, peck them out. In the end I thought of my parents…how upset they'd be. But I wasn't sad to leave this world. This world where people see you dying, and all they do is watch from the safety of the deck. A world where soldiers bomb innocent women and children…a world where the ones at the top know a German submarine is going to intercept your passenger ship – and they let it happen for their own despicable ends. They're all as wicked as each other. I know that now. I'm just glad to be out of it.

I tried to loosen my lifebelt. But I couldn't. My fingers were too stiff. And when you can't do that, it takes a long time to die…feels like days…and nights and nights…

DEATH IN AN AIRSHIP

For the first time in history, civilians are to be targeted from the air.

A small BOY of around 12 years old (DEATH.) enters with a large black balloon on a string.

BOY: I first saw an airship in 1907 and my granddad told me all about Count Zeppelin. In the Franco-Prussian war Granddad was famous as a scout, and he used to follow the French army, spying on them for days. Well, we won't need to do that anymore, Granddad. Airships are the scouts now. And they're too high up away for enemy guns.

In 1909 the French had five military aeroplanes. The Germans laughed at them and called them 'crazy'. But five years later the Germans had aeroplanes too, and they soon discovered a horrible fact – a plane can rip an airship and send it burning to the ground. But an airship can't rip a plane.

I want to be a pilot when I grow up.

I once had a ride on the airship Luise. Luise was paid for by the army, but they never wanted airships. But the people did, and 78 were built by popular demand. 52 burned up during the war, most of them over London. My dad says, even though airships are death traps, public opinion got its way.

The aeroplanes could never carry enough bombs. They would have to be as big as airships, and airships had vanished before the end of the war because they were so big.

Experts say that planes can't drop bombs. I don't think I believe them. Dad says he's never met an expert who wasn't an idiot.

And actually, the French dropped bombs from aeroplanes in 1916 and kill 82 children in an orphanage. The Germans learnt even more worse things were needed. Poison gas – that's a German invention!

SCENE 9
A SCIENTIST FAILS
Faradeyweg 8. Dahlem, Berlin
2 May 1915

A service villa belonging to one of the directors of the Kaiser Wilhelm Institute: dark brown panelling up to the ceiling, little stucco, bookshelves with glass doors built into the walls in the library of this scholarly couple. There is an institutional oppressive feeling to the room, rather like a prison, which is in essence, what is was.

The director is DR FRITZ HABER, a professor at the university. He is married to DR CLARA IMMERWAHR, the first woman to graduate from the University of Breslau with a degree in chemistry.

CLARA is 43 years old. She is wearing, as was fashionable among intellectual women around 1910, what were known as 'reformation clothes'.

HABER is bald, wears a pince-nez, an upturned collar, and the 'dirty nose' (the colloquial name for the moustache). He also wears a white coat, under which are the military clothes and boots he will soon wear in the War. He has an Iron Cross, First Class.

A lectern sits atop a large worktable covered in books and papers. The HABERS work next to each other, though somewhat separated.

CLARA abandons what she is writing and turns to her husband. He is in the process of writing something down. She speaks aggressively.

CLARA: You seem to think I'm one of your students! I don't expect patriotic platitudes from a scientist. Preachers, yes! They have no evidence to prove their case, so they fall back on emotion. But you! You don't need to, so don't fob me off with all that nonsense! Poison gas against unprotected people! It's immoral!

HABER: *(Initially in measured tones, but then more agitated.)* The soldiers have to have the weapons that the enemy will soon have too. No country has a monopoly on weaponry.

CLARA: Fritz, you've already done all you can for the fatherland. When the admiral's staff couldn't get sulphur from Chile anymore, you saved their skins, so they could still use the guns. What you did then was legitimate. Gas isn't!

HABER: *(Sarcastically, almost arrogantly.)* What is legitimate in war?

CLARA: Making sure your own weapons are as effective as the enemy's. But chlorine gas is another matter. Our enemies don't have it.

HABER: Not yet, Clara! If we don't surprise them, they will surprise us! *(Deeply hurt.)* Would you call the man a criminal who first fired cannonballs against knights in armour? Is it the choice of weapon that makes war moral or amoral? To choke on gas is no worse than bleeding to death from a bullet. And everyone has bullets, of course. So more people die when both sides fight with the same weapons. But if we can surprise the enemy, we'll win the war, there'll be much less bloodshed.

CLARA steps away from the lectern. She pushes the books so forcefully that they fall off the table.

CLARA: So it's a question of speed, nothing more. Really easy! I've had enough! You can find another assistant.

HABER: Clara, you were never my assistant. You were always my partner. I always praised you as such, told people you were the first woman to get a chemistry doctorate from Breslau. *(He picks up the books, shouts at her.)* But all this now! You are acting like an assistant!

CLARA: *(Speaking as if in a dream.)* That time we were walking by the lake… Hermann was still in his pram… I remember saying that in future wars chemistry and biology would help to avoid the destruction of buildings…of anything material. You were horrified! But now that the sky is full of airships and half the North Sea hidden in smoke, and you can drop bacteria on the other countries, you want to do it. Six months ago, I'd have hit anyone who said you'd do what you are doing today. You had feelings for other people once. Not any more!

HABER: *(Calmly, convinced that his conscience is clear.)* That's a bit strong, Clara!

CLARA: You think so? You used to help people – the fertilizer that rescued the farmers from ruin; the firedamp detector that saved miners' lives. But now chemical warfare!

She sobs, sits down.

HABER: *(Going to her, putting his hand to her hair.)* If the fatherland needs me now, how am I to blame? Time and geography, Clara. They are just like fate. But you, Clara, you are so self-righteous! Would you say the inventor of gunpowder is responsible for 400 years of war? I can't think why we are even discussing this. Go and ask our friends what they think. See if they blame me too.

CLARA: *(Scornfully.)* I imagine you've already won them over, Otto Hahn especially.

HABER: Do you think he wouldn't agree with me, especially after Sackur was killed, trying to put chlorine gas into grenades?

CLARA: *(Laughs.)* I'm sorry, Fritz! When you and Sackur were working together and the gas killed him, he deserved it!

HABER: Like I said, Clara, your self-righteousness is unbelievable!

CLARA: Really? You think it acceptable that you, my husband, the father of my son...

HABER: Our son, if you don't mind.

CLARA: ...is making one of the deadliest weapons ever created? And you try to excuse yourself by talking about the inventor of gunpowder!

HABER nervously takes the pince-nez from his nose and polishes the lenses vigorously, attempting to mask his anger:

HABER: So what is it you want me to do?

CLARA: Stop experimenting with chlorine gas! Doctors take the Hippocratic oath. Chemists do not. But there are unwritten laws of humanity. If you don't stop, I promise you, I'm leaving.

HABER: I took an oath to my Kaiser and my country – to use my knowledge as best I can.

CLARA: Why not conscience too?

HABER: I do have a conscience, Clara. That's why I offer the fatherland a weapon that can end the war. I mean really end it.

CLARA: *(Calm and composed.)* In that case, I'm leaving.

HABER has been experiencing these confrontations for months, and for that reason can make sensible suggestions.

HABER: Clara, soldiers at the front…they have to do without their wives. But tell me this: should they have to do without a weapon that could save their lives, just because I don't want you to leave? The answer's simple. You can go. But take Hermann with you. Stay in Switzerland for as long as the war lasts. I'll try to get you a visa.

CLARA: *(As if she has come to a decision.)* I can't take him with me…

HABER: You have to. There are good schools. If you leave him here, who takes care of his schooling?

CLARA: *(Close to tears.)* Hermann stays with you. There's nothing more to say.

HABER: *(Writing something down, somewhat distracted.)* In that case I'll get Sackur's daughter to look after him. Since her father died, she's got no money, not even her father's pension.

CLARA: *(Sarcastically.)* You seem very concerned about her. Maybe you fancy her. Very well, go ahead. Employ the girl. Get her a job at the Institute too! Otherwise, she'll just be a maid…and a mistress, of course.

HABER: *(Shrugging.)* You don't really believe that! Anyway, where are you thinking of going?

CLARA: *(As if talking about the weather.)* I don't know. But I'm not taking Hermann…not if I decide to end it all.

HABER: Alright! When Germany's no longer in danger, we can separate without any fuss.

CLARA: Fine! As long as you don't think I'll come back when you ride in triumph through the Brandenburg Gate…the Kaiser's pet scientist!

HABER: I didn't ask for that! It was just a matter of making explosives another way. Still, I have to accept that I'm the only German whose wife is leaving him because he's involved in the war! I suppose you look down on the women who stay with their husbands, knowing that they've killed others.

CLARA: There is a difference. The soldier in the trenches is forced to kill. If he doesn't, he'll be killed. And if he refuses to fight, he'll be shot by his own people.

HABER: So if I volunteer for the Front, you'll stay with me!

CLARA: Oh, yes. I'm sure you'd do that! You think they'd accept you at forty-five? No one kills the goose that lays the golden egg. So either you stop this work, or I shall do what I say.

HABER: Clara, please! You love our son as much as I do. You think he could cope with his mother killing herself? He's only twelve years old! Listen…we'll invite Otto Hahn and his wife to dinner, talk all this through… But I do have to go to the Institute now… I'll be back this afternoon.

He has already looked at his pocket watch three times.

CLARA: I shan't be here this afternoon.

HABER: *(Going out.)* I have to put on my uniform. I'll be back in a moment. Where is Hermann now?

CLARA: *(Sarcastically.)* Why ask? You never ask. He's outside, down by the lake.

HABER: *(Half way through the door.)* Perhaps he ought to spend more time with you.

CLARA: Don't bring him into this. In any case, we are just as helpless as any child.

HABER: I'm sorry. I have to go.

CLARA: Of course you do!

He exits.

Such consideration!

She opens the lectern and produces a pistol. She releases the safety catch.

CLARA: If I don't do it now, he'll take the pistol! I need to be sure where Hermann is.

She goes to the window.

CLARA: He's outside!… God! I can't look at him!

She turns away from the window, steps forward, shoots herself in the chest and falls onto the long table.

HABER, dressed now in a grey field uniform, his Iron Cross on his chest, his cap on his head, rushes in. He falls to his knees, places a hand under CLARA's head, lifts her a little. He is unable to speak.

DO NOT OBEY

For the first time we see the new German army's steel helmet: not spiked but smooth, extending into the back of the neck. It is a helmet similar to the one that Hitler's army still wore, except that on each side it reaches down to the top of the ear.

In field grey, short dirty boots, fresh from the battle, for the first time DEATH allows the body he has inhabited to speak:

SOLDIER: Can't see, can't think. Running. Terror. Heart racing. Hell erupting – then. Suddenly. The world. Stops. Fragments. Disappears. And I am engulfed in…light. Silence. Time – stretches. The light is inside me – and I am dissolving and my last thought is – so this is what it's like. Heaven. And I feel – joy.

Breath. In. Blackness. Falling. Mud. Bombs. Dirt. Flying. Landing. Shooting. Shouting. Limbs wrenched. I'm screaming. Arms pinned – caught in a trap. I look down. My leg is gone. A black, ragged, bleeding fleshy stump pissing blood. And I'm caught. On wire. Arms spread wide. Pinned Like a rat impaled for dissection. Guts hanging out. But. I'm alive. I feel a barbarian, primal. Agony. An unstoppable white-hot wave courses through me. I vomit. Bullets flying past me. Slam into me. Torment beyond anything I have words for. Then I hear a strange, guttural sound. And I realise. It's me. I'm beyond screaming. Beyond anything. I just hang there. It feels like hours but it can't be. The pain has driven me from my mind. And then – suddenly – nothing.

I'm awake. There's no pain. I'm in a box. And the air is corrupt with…the smell of shit. I open my eyes. Panic. Then I understand. It's me. Rotting. I am here. And I am not here. I am dead. And I am not dead.

Twenty-first of February. 1916. Four fifteen.

I didn't know the kind of warfare we learned about as children, the glory, the heroism had ended. And something else had begun.

Our masters called it – Material Battle. We were the material. There to be thrown into their bloody inferno. Like you'd throw coal into a fire. I was a lump of coal.

And like all good Germans, I believed what I was told: that France had declared war.

They demanded we take Verdun, that impregnable fortress 'Fight or I'll strike you dead. Obey!' they said. So we did. We kissed our families. Our children. Promised we'd be home.

Two and a half million shells rained down on Verdun. The sky was black with them. Death, upon death upon death.

We thought we were to capture the fortress. What we didn't know was that Falkenhayn, the Kaiser's Chief of Staff, had other ideas. He didn't want Verdun. He wanted attack, attack, attack. As long as the French had reserves, attack. Take as many of their lives as we could – attack. That was the his plan.

But France didn't fall. Nothing. Was. Gained.

Falkenhayn was removed. But while the battle raged on, we dead rose to speak. But we couldn't make the living hear us. Couldn't make them mutiny. Couldn't make them turn their guns on the guilty.

So I find no rest. I lie in the bitter fluids of unsatisfied vengeance and rise and walk with my torment held fast behind. I failed in life; I fail in death. I failed to kill even one of the guilty.

The Generals never heard the screams of the dying. Never saw the corpses piled up.

Had I taken even one. It would have given meaning to my life, memory to my name. Ended my torment here.

Listen to us. Listen to those whose children have no father. Listen to those whose wives have no husband. Listen to me when I say: when you know they're sending you to certain death. Do not obey. Do not die wretchedly as I died. Do not be their Material. We who die should have meaning to our deaths. You can't have meaning if you obey. You can't kill the guilty if you obey. So never obey. Never obey. Do not obey. Never obey.

He walks off, still repeating 'Never obey', fading into the mist, the sound of the battle continues.

SCENE 10
Now Thank We All Our God
Ministry of War, Berlin
4 August 1914

A balcony room – as large as a hall – in the Berlin palace, the room to the balcony from which KAISER WILHELM, the last Kaiser, declared a state of war with the memorably famous phrase: 'From now on, I recognize no parties – only Germans.' It inspired the people beneath the balcony – 30,000, though other estimates suggest twice that number – to start singing vigorously the hymn 'Now Thank We All Our God', to which this final scene of the Dance of Death refers, and which swells to the volume of the music at the beginning of this play on the Isle of Death. It is now played over a war zone.

The Germans who have so far appeared on stage (excluding the HABERs) will one by one appear again: the Chancellor BETHMANN-HOLLWEG; the Foreign Secretary JAGOW; the Editor of the Berliner Tageblatt, DR WOLFF; the artist WILLY STÖWER, who will paint the scene; Chief of Staff GENERAL MOLTKE and His Majesty's Secretary of State of the German Imperial Navy GRAND ADMIRAL TIRPITZ. The KAISER has not entered yet.

The back wall of the almost empty hall is decorated only with a rug and two chandeliers. Most of the space is taken up by the windows to the left and right of the wide balcony doors, which will be opened only later, when the KAISER goes out to announce to his people that war has finally broken out. A table sits centrally draped in Imperial Blue baise and covered with maps of the empire.

Now only BETHMANN and GENERAL MOLTKE are on stage. MOLTKE, even though it is warm outside, is wearing his helmet.

Like most things here, this is totally insane, but real enough. This last day of peace in the German camp (Austria has already advanced on Belgrade) is possibly, in all its dramatic absurdity, the blackest comedy in history.

Our scene begins at 18:30 on a cloudless summer evening.

BETHMANN inclines his head a little towards the Chief of Staff MOLTKE, offering his congratulations.

MOLTKE: It's quite an achievement, Excellency, to get his Majesty prepared for war. You'll go down in history as the first German chancellor brave enough to march against Russia and France.

BETHMANN smiles – he wants to be seen as a diplomatic genius.

BETHMANN: *(Mollified and flattered.)* Quite possibly, Moltke, but the Kaiser has yet to sign the order for mobilisation.

MOLTKE: But he can't change his mind at this stage… How did you convince him to go ahead?

BETHMANN: *(Seriously.)* I received a telegram saying that London would become involved if we did not negotiate with them. But I kept this from His Majesty.

MOLTKE: Without your intervention he would have backed down again?

BETHMANN: I think so.

MOLTKE: *(Excited.)* We all know the British have no intention of negotiating. They simply want to buy time… They want us to believe that the Russians are only concerned with Austria. It's ludicrous, given that Churchill has already prepared his fleet.

BETHMANN: Still, I have to say that perhaps we should have accepted London's offer of a conference of four – though victory would more than make up for it.

MOLTKE: The General Staff is convinced we shouldn't move against Russia. We need to deal with France first.

BETHMANN becomes caught up in the excitement. He already sees how he is being drawn into the trap of his own intrigues, which are leading to the instigation of the war.

BETHMANN: *(Grabbing MOLTKE by the sleeve.)* The French will not declare war on us unless we do so on Russia, in which case to attack France is out of the question. They haven't even mobilised. So it has to be Russia.

MOLTKE is completely horrified. He is guilty of a very serious omission of duty as Chief of Staff, for he has not come up with an alternative to the Schlieffen Plan of attack since Schlieffen's retirement in 1906. In the event of France not becoming involved in the war, he has not even considered the possibility of marching on the East.

MOLTKE: But Chancellor! An attack on Russia will stop us dealing with France!

BETHMANN: How else can we start this war? You've been wanting it for the past year. Do you have a plan other than the Schlieffen Plan to attack France first?

MOLTKE: *(His voice small, like that of a petty thief caught in the act.)* No. I'm afraid I don't.

BETHMANN's fear that MOLTKE has no alternative to the invasion of France turns his laugh into a roar.

BETHMANN: Then how the hell do we force France's hand if we don't attack Russia first?

MOLTKE: Allow me to say, sir, that neither you nor His Majesty ever toyed with the idea of a war against Russia. Not unless France was involved.

BETHMANN: I agree.

MOLTKE: So what if they don't want to be involved? We could seize the moment, now or never!

BETHMANN: Allow me, Moltke, to play devil's advocate for a moment. What if someone had convinced the Kaiser to declare war on Russia first?

MOLTKE: Then Russia would be forced to mobilise. They would be the aggressor.

BETHMANN: Then we could mobilise too.

A SERVANT enters, about to announce JAGOW, but JAGOW announces himself. At the same time, TIRPITZ, STÖWER and WOLFF enter.

JAGOW: *(Calling out as he enters.)* It seems his Majesty has some excellent news!

He directs the remark to BETHMANN, his superior, but before he can say any more, the KAISER himself enters.

The SERVANT closes the door but stays inside.

JAGOW hands BETHMANN a telegram from London. The civilians – JAGOW, STÖWER and WOLFF – bow so low they seem in danger of performing a somersault. BETHMANN, TIRPITZ, MOLTKE are standing to attention.

Those in uniform salute: MOLTKE, a hand to his spiked helmet; TIRPITZ to his bicorn; BETHMANN to his grey one. The KAISER, when he is in civilian dress or in his uniform and without the sabre, always places his left hand on (not in) the pocket of his frockcoat.

The KAISER now seems full of hope. BETHMANN gives the telegram to TIRPITZ, who takes it with his left hand because he is saluting with the right.

KAISER: Gentlemen, France is abandoning Russia. She will not be declaring war. And I understand from the British Foreign Secretary that England will not be joining in, provided we only march on Russia. We shall enjoy a splendid victory! It calls for champagne all round!

The SERVANT exits, after life-threatening bow.

MOLTKE steps forward boldly, but – before he can utter a word – TIRPITZ interrupts, stroking his beard and full of self-importance.

TIRPITZ: In my opinion, your Majesty, England is afraid to test her fleet against your own. Too much of a risk.

MOLTKE: *(Interrupting TIRPITZ.)* I have to say, your Majesty… if the Schlieffen Plan is abandoned in favour of an advance on Russia alone, you will not have a competent army – more a disorganized mob. No road map, no marching orders, no supplies, no trains, no horses, no weapons! If the Plan is not put into effect…

KAISER: For God's sake, man! Schlieffen died in 1905. The plan is old hat!

MOLTKE: Your Majesty, a march on Russia is still far too risky…

KAISER: Tell me something, Moltke, did you ever consider such a campaign?

MOLTKE: I did not, your Majesty. You once informed my General Staff that such a campaign was impossible.

KAISER: But answer the question: did the General Staff ever consider a campaign which involved Russia but not France?

MOLTKE: *(Meekly.)* Yes, your Majesty. Three years ago. We rejected it.

KAISER: *(Annoyed.)* Your predecessor would have answered differently. He would not have put all his eggs in one basket. What do you do all day in the General Staff? Twiddle your fingers?

MOLTKE: Allow me to point out, your Majesty, that you yourself believed a war involving both was something to be feared.

KAISER: *(Gruffly, because he is afraid.)* Feared? Why feared? We are not afraid! So…move your troops to the West if you wish, but then you turn them around, march to the East. There will be no war with France unless I say so, no advance on Luxembourg.

The SERVANT enters with champagne. He carries the bottle in a napkin, and is accompanied by a very young man. Both are wearing white gloves, the younger one balancing a large silver salver with 12 empty flutes and also an ice-bucket containing a second bottle of champagne.

They both stand to attention, first before the KAISER, then before BETHMANN. They pour the champagne and each gentleman takes his glass. MOLTKE has fallen silent at the KAISER's refusal to enter Luxembourg. TIRPITZ steps forward, his white-gloved hand at his bicorn.

TIRPITZ: Allow me to offer an opinion, your Majesty. As far as France is concerned, I think we should wait until France declares war on us, not the other way round. If we attack the French, England will be obliged to honour its treaty with them.

MOLTKE: 'Wait' you say! Wait for what? The Russians have already mobilised! But perhaps your Majesty prefers not to declare war on either! We could abandon war altogether!

He laughs as if this was incredibly unreasonable, but the KAISER replies sombrely and quietly:

KAISER: Yes, why not, Julius? Cheers! Neither France nor England has given any indication that they will invade us.

TIRPITZ: Your Majesty... I rather think that the English and French positions may be intended to deceive us. When we have sent our army deep into Russia, the French will advance across the Rhine...

MOLTKE: *(Interrupting.)* Which is why we should get a guarantee from the French that they will not do so if we do not threaten them.

The KAISER has never heard of such a possibility. In his view, MOLTKE is an airhead.

KAISER: What kind of guarantee, Moltke? What guarantee can we ask of a country that's done us no harm? One moment, please! Inform her Majesty and the Crown Prince that we'd like them to join us! Thank you!

The KAISER may have said this to the SERVANTS in order to get rid of them. He doesn't want them to hear the argument.

SERVANT: Yes, sir! At once, sir!

Both exit quickly.

KAISER: *(Poking STÖWER with his cane.)* I can see you can't wait to start sketching. Why not begin?

STÖWER: *(Standing to attention.)* Thank you, your Majesty.

He fetches a chair, slips off his shoes, spreads a handkerchief on the chair and sits on the handkerchief.

The KAISER addresses DR WOLFF, who has held up his notepad just as STÖWER has held up a sketchbook to get the KAISER's attention.

KAISER: Dr Wolff, please check with General Moltke and the Chancellor before you put anything in the newspaper.

WOLFF: I shall, your Majesty. Thank you.

KAISER: We've had no censorship here to date. Long may it continue! Now – back to the guarantee, Moltke... What did you have in mind?

All this happens very quickly. There is hardly any interruption of the military conversation. WOLFF has moved away from the military men. He leans against the window while making notes.

MOLTKE: It has to be something, your Majesty, that the French are bound to refuse.

KAISER: *(Sick of MOLTKE.)* Yes, yes, Moltke. But what kind of guarantee is that? Be more specific!

MOLTKE: Your Majesty could ask the French to open up their strongest forts to us, Verdun, Belfort, Toul… If we guarantee not to march against Paris.

KAISER: Should we include the Eiffel Tower too, Julius?

He points his finger to his head, as if to say that MOLTKE is crazy.

If the French Foreign Minister agreed to such a demand, he'd be shot outright. Your plans are poppycock. Be realistic!

BETHMANN: *(Wanting to be seen as bold.)* Your Majesty, I agree with General Moltke. Make the demand impossible and France will be forced to declare war.

KAISER: But why encourage a war on two fronts? Russia is surely enough, even if Moltke has no other plan in mind.

BETHMANN: As far as England is concerned, your Majesty, her offer of negotiation should be rejected. Any agreement might lead to fewer ships being built.

KAISER: *(Becoming heated.)* I can't see how you reach that conclusion, Chancellor. No one dictates how many ships I build.

BETHMANN: *(Bowing.)* Indeed, your Majesty. I agree.

The SERVANT now returns, salutes, and then wordlessly hands the KAISER a sealed message.

The KAISER has read the telegram. But, before he can speak, MOLTKE loses his nerve, and is very close to tears. Outraged, he cries out with more determination than he will ever reveal again:

MOLTKE: Your Majesty, I repeat – I will not be responsible for a war that does not include the invasion of France!

KAISER: Well, it seems things have come to a head. I'm told here that the French have ordered mobilisation. We are justified. Russia and France both mobilising ahead of Germany!

The KAISER *prudently conceals the fact that several hours ago –
together with* BETHMANN *and behind the back of the generals –
he ordered the German ambassador to Petersburg to declare war
on the Russians, Russia not having responded to his ultimatum
that they should call off their mobilisation. The fact that German
mobilisation only came after the Russian one was kept secret in
London and Paris.*

KAISER: So we don't need to be shy. I shall sign the
mobilisation order. Open the balcony windows! The
people outside…they can barely contain their enthusiasm!
(To the SERVANT.) First Foot Guards uniform, please!

SERVANT bows, exits.

SERVANT: At once, your Majesty! Uniform, First Foot Guards.

KAISER: *(To the assembled men.)* Prepare an answer for me to
the King of England. I wish to thank him for the British
intending to remain neutral.

BETHMANN: Your Majesty, it seems to me that King George is
merely *considering* neutrality.

*BETHMANN hands the KAISER a golden pen with which he will
sign the order for mobilisation. JAGOW has already excused himself
and gone to the adjoining room, and returns with a large red leather
folder which BETHMANN unlocks with the key on his long keychain
and places in front of the KAISER: the certificate, the signing of which
signifies the implementation of mobilisation.*

*All stand at attention and watch – those in uniform saluting – as the
two SERVANTS spread out the golden writing material on the desk.
JAGOW clears STÖWER from the chair and brings it for the KAISER,
but he signs standing up, bending over the table.*

We now hear the nationalistic baying of the people in front
of the palace. Someone has started singing 'The Watch
Guard on the Rhine', which is then taken up by the crowd.

KAISER: *(Straightens up.)* Now, gentlemen. Deal with the
answer to the King of England. Thank him on my behalf…
Next door, if you don't mind. I have to put on my First
Foot Guards uniform. No King of Prussia has declared war
without it.

All jump to it. The civilians, bowing and scraping, exit. Only TIRPITZ *remains at the door.*

TIRPITZ: Allow me, your Majesty, to recall the words of Leopold von Ranke. They will give you and your people the required strength in this undertaking: 'It is the fate of all peoples to ripen and evolve through sea voyage and war'.

He bows. The KAISER *goes over to him, but before he can embrace him,* TIRPITZ *leans forward to kiss his hand.*

KAISER: Thank you, Tirpitz. God preserve all German sailors!

TIRPITZ exits. Both SERVANTS return with the Prussian-blue uniform of the First Foot Guards.

The KAISER *removes his jacket, which has been unbuttoned for him and the cords loosened. He is silent, and one can hear 'The Watch Guard on the Rhine' being sung from below.*

WOLFF enters hurriedly. The young man is timid because the KAISER *is in his undergarments and shirtsleeves. He steps back, shocked to have discovered his monarch like this.*

KAISER: *(Cheerfully.)* Oh, come here, man! Have you never seen bare legs before?

WOLFF: I was told to bring this quickly, your Majesty.

KAISER: *(Amused.)* Yes, yes. Open it!

Because he is still being dressed, he is unable to open the telegram himself. WOLFF opens it instead.

The KAISER *takes the telegram from him. He reads it. His face reveals a sense of shock.*

KAISER: Get me the Chancellor!

WOLFF: Yes, sir. The Chancellor!

He hurries to the room next door. The SERVANTS dress the KAISER in his uniform. They put on his sabre and hand him the spiked helmet. He doesn't take it yet. Instead, he stares ahead, while the SERVANTS hang his previous uniform from a clothes rack.

BETHMANN: *(Entering.)* Your Majesty!

It costs the KAISER *a great effort to articulate his first few words. He tries to hand the telegram to* BETHMANN *but it falls on the carpet. BETHMANN, aware of the KAISER's sense of shock, picks up the telegram.*

The KAISER struggles to get his breath, and sits.

KAISER: We need a miracle! A telegram from the King of England. It says they cannot remain neutral.

BETHMANN does not dare read the telegram while the KAISER is speaking. Now he does so.

The SERVANT gives the KAISER his golden cigarette case.

BETHMANN: A surprise, your Majesty! *(He looks for a scapegoat.)* We obviously fell for the English trap.

KAISER: Hardly surprising when we're dealing with scoundrels. So what should I do? Send a message to my cousin George? Tell him we'll negotiate if he can persuade the Russians to stop their mobilisation?

Only now can the KAISER take a cigarette and have it lit.

JAGOW has now entered. He has heard the last few words. BETHMANN hands him the telegram. JAGOW has taken in the content of the telegram in one glance. BETHMANN is lost for words.

So the 'encirclement' of Germany has come to fruition! We should admire it even if it destroys us. Carelessness and weakness will be responsible for this terrible war. England, Russia and France have agreed amongst themselves to use the Austro-Serbian conflict as an excuse to wage war on us. They aim to satisfy their envy by destroying us. You people in the Foreign Office! You must have been asleep! It should not have come to this! I must address the people.

BETHMANN: Your Majesty! I wish to resign. We have our part in the responsibility for this war. I ask to step down as Chancellor.

The KAISER looks as if he is about to hit BETHMANN with his field marshal's stick. Instead, he puts his spiked helmet on and prepares to exit.

KAISER: You will stay, Bethmann. You make your bed, you lie on it!

JAGOW indicates to the SERVANT that he should fetch the people from the adjoining room. BETHMANN bows in response to the KAISER's rejection of his offer of resignation.

The people enter from the other room.

The KAISER goes out onto the balcony, beneath which there are those Berliners who do not work during the day but have time to rush to the palace and wait there for hours for the appearance of the KAISER. Thousands begin to intone 'Deutschland, Deutschland, über alles', but then break off. Some stragglers continue, but then stop because they see that the KAISER is about to speak.

But before he has stepped out onto the balcony, BETHMANN has summoned the others. JAGOW, TIRPITZ and MOLTKE are informed of the bad news by a fearful BETHMANN.

BETHMANN: A telegram from the King of England. Her neutrality is not, after all, guaranteed. Our ambassador must have misunderstood.

JAGOW throws his arms in the air but says nothing. He goes out onto the balcony. National fervour (a flattering description of animal cries) expresses itself in 'hurrahs' and bursts of the national anthem. As they fade, the KAISER is able to speak.

The two civilians, WOLFF and STÖWER approach the balcony but keep their distance. STÖWER is to sketch the scene and WOLFF to describe it.

STÖWER: We are truly blessed, Doctor Wolff! I never imagined that in our lifetime we would experience a great sea-battle against perfidious Albion.

WOLFF: I'm not so sure, Mr Stöwer. You know what the Spaniards say: 'War with the world but peace with England'. For the last few days can't get it out of my head.

He goes past the painter to the balcony door but does not step out. The KAISER has already started speaking. STÖWER takes a chair and stands on it. He starts sketching from behind those on the balcony.

The KAISER begins his speech. It is only partly true, but extremely convincing.

KAISER: I thank you all for the love and loyalty you have shown me in the last few days. They were days the like of which we have never seen! If this should now come to war, there will be no political parties. They may all have attacked me in the past, but that was in peacetime. Today I forgive them wholeheartedly. Today we are all German brothers, German brothers only. So now I believe you should go to your churches, kneel before God, and pray that He helps our brave men in the conflict that lies ahead. We will defend ourselves to the last man. We shall resist our enemies. When Germany is united, it is never defeated!

Somebody below calls out 'Now Thank We All Our God' and the crowd takes it up. The beginning of the hymn drags a little, but is already quite loud and then picks up, as if someone is conducting.

Suddenly, in the middle of the room, we see the figure of DEATH. He raises his hand to the palace servant, indicating that he should leave...

THE UNKNOWN SOLDIER

DEATH: You, to the Front!

The old man cringes in horror. He staggers away. DEATH turns and addresses the other men.

DEATH: You, to the Front! You too! And you! And you!

WOLFF and STÖWER continue to work as if DEATH isn't there.

The KAISER re-enters to the sound of cheering outside. It's as if WOLFF and STÖWER are in a different reality, still sketching the KAISER outside.

The KAISER re-enters to the sound of cheering outside.

KAISER: *(To DEATH.)* Get me some champagne. Did you hear me, scoundrel? Bow before me!

DEATH merely smiles at him.

KAISER: Do I know you, man?

DEATH: Oh certainly you'll come to
With you I'll do my job
Personally.
Far from the carnage of the cutting machine.

KAISER: What balderdash is this?

DEATH: Even in these straitened times
When I am all but done for
I can still take one soul
And it's fitting that like me you'll come
Deposed
Exiled
Put out to pasture before your time.

KAISER: Poppycock! Are you mad?

DEATH: For four long years you'll spill the blood,
    The blood of people who don't matter.
    While you and your kind stay clear of bullets,
    Far from the death rattle machine-gun fire
    The generals, all safe and sound,
    Will send to doom nine million men
    Men they'll never see or know,
    Who'll blindly obey their feckless commands.

KAISER: Do you know who I am? I am the grandson of
    Frederick Wilhelm, the Great Elector!
    Stop this at once! Get out of my sight!

DEATH: And in the battle's senseless rush,
    They'll die in tortured agony,
    And will their death be recognised?
    Not in the pages of your history!
    They're just cards in a senseless game,
    Where generals bleat and blather.
    So what shall we call this unknown man?
    Let's call him the unknown soldier.

KAISER: I will have you shot.

DEATH: And you will flee. No more Berlin
    You'll be beaten, but no suicide!
    You're the worst kind of person,
    Living a coward – exiled!
    And meanwhile
    Your palaces, like coffins,
    Will lie, unused
    No one wants you or yours
    You'll suffer, look
    At every corpse with envy,
    But you'll have to wait your turn
    Twenty long years you'll be king of nothing

KAISER: Guards!

DEATH: It's too late for that.

    He lifts his head – simultaneously, WOLFF and STÖWER theirs.

DEATH: Shhh. Listen – can you hear?
    The cutting machine has begun –

Here it comes. I have work to do – I really must be off.

DEATH begins to sing. As the song progresses, he begins to shed the mantle of the SERVANT, and by the end, he is very clearly DEATH at his most hideous and frightening.

Simultaneously, WOLFF and STÖWER assist DEATH in his song. Meanwhile, DEATH engages the baffled KAISER in his routine throughout.

The stage becomes darker and darker, as the song takes us from life to the Underworld. At the end, DEATH seats the KAISER at his desk.

DEATH: To those in the high command
We all just pawns in their game.
Soldier, sailor, it makes no difference,
In death one and all are all the same.

Newspapers laud their victories,
Admirals, generals all,
But you, anonymous soldier,
They don't give a damn where you fall.

The further they are from the murder,
The more they puff out their chest,
The greater the glint of their medals,
Pinned to their cold-hearted breasts.

For them we're just cannon-fodder,
Just a way to show off the flag,
While we the young are bleeding,
Sewn into body-bags.
While we the young lie dying
Sewn into body bags.

NEKROLOGUE

DEATH: And so this bloody war begins
Why does God allow it?
He'll ignore their pleas
When they turn to Him
While the ones who deny that the crime
Was theirs
Will claim it's only God's will
You think this road, soaked in blood,

Has anything to do with God?
God made the world and now says nothing.
Silence his revenge for this bloody mess.
And oh how amusing
They've called on me, the weapons men
Whose designs are used for a million deaths
They long for an end to their leaders
Who have turned their little games to war
Yet it's them who made it possible,
To bring the dead here in droves
Men are falling by their thousands,
And those in power cling to all they've conquered?
Listen…

VOICE OF THE KAISER: The battle is won, the English totally defeated…champagne!… When an English parliamentarian comes to beg for peace, he shall kneel before the Imperial standard. This is the victory of monarchy over democracy!

DEATH: This is from the day Germany will stop
This round of bloodshed and admit defeat.
Yet the Kaiser calls for champagne as his soldiers fall
Just hours before the death knell, he claims victory.
Deluded megalomaniac!
He never saw a military hospital,
The victims of his war,
Waiting for a bed in which to die
He and all his thugs. Think only of their profits
Their medals, even when
The carnage claims their sons.

In the hospitals the fallen plead with God,
Scream beneath their bandages,
I cannot bear the sight of it
Listen to this! Two dying horses, badly wounded

A horse screams.
A boy lying in no-man's-land, not yet twenty…

The dying man screams for his mother.
Listen! The barracks in Flanders!

Men crying, screaming.

Listen! A child behind blockades dying of starvation!
A terrible groaning begins.
And God allows this!

And in twenty years, another war,
Like bombs exploding, fireworks firing
It ignites! This second from the first!
The Austrian marches into Paris
There's Auswitzch Birkenau, Belsen Belsen
Belsec, Dachau, Dunkirk,
Siberia, Stalin's bloody massacre
And so it ignites and ignites again
Korea, Vietnam, Nigeria
Congo, Bosnia, Sudan,
Afghanistan, Iran-Iraq

And so it will go on,
Ignite ignite ignite
Until there's just one more,
The masterpiece to the end all wars
Human beings chose this path
I never hurt anybody! God is silent!
This is them! All them!

You hear it? The cutting machine
Comes and comes again!
Then I'll play the part
They long for!
Put them out of their misery!
Bring the airplanes! Bombers! Tanks! Jets! Satellites!
Napalm, nitro, chemicals, viruses,
Stealth bombs, dirty bombs, smart bombs, trident
Bring them!
War heads, star wars, fusion, destruction
Bring the light!
Bring the light!
Bring the blinding light!
Drop the bombs!
Drop the bomb!
Let them scream it was I who did them a better service
than their God!

We hear the voices of war: snippets of speeches made by Hitler at Nuremburg, the voices of those men who ordered the troops into Vietnam, Iraq, Afghanistan, etc.

Their voices mix with the sounds of the killing machines and the ever-evolving sounds of war, as DEATH gives up hope, he turns his anger directly to the audience. His screams and the noise becomes an explosion so strong the entire theatre seems to be torn apart.

END.

WWW.OBERONBOOKS.COM

Follow us on www.twitter.com/@oberonbooks
& www.facebook.com/oberonbook